This is a wonderful book, full of bil
and theological depth. It is a great
alism, selfishness and consumerism
world into our church. It encourages us to be the church we believe
in and want to belong to.

Peter Adam
Vicar Emeritus, St Jude's Carlton, Melbourne
Former Principal, Ridley College, Melbourne

A clear and compelling book about the church, carefully grounded
in the word and insightfully applied to our world. Deenick inspires
us with God's glorious vision for the church, prepares us for challenges and struggles that we will encounter, and equips us to be
what God calls us to be. Read this book, and be excited about the
church!

Derek Brotherson
Principal, Sydney Missionary and Bible College

Church is, or should be, a big part of the lives of all Christians.
But many turn up without thinking very clearly, biblically or practically about what church is all about. This great little book will
help them do exactly that. Deeply rooted in Scripture, it is a crystal clear, deeply challenging and wonderfully refreshing guide to
living in God's church today. I'd love to see everyone who goes to
church read it—they and their churches will benefit greatly.

Murray Capill
Dean of Ministry Development, Reformed Theological
College, Melbourne

Arguably the greatest challenge the pandemic has brought to the church has been in people's understanding of the purpose and importance of church itself. Against this background, Karl Deenick takes us carefully through the Bible's teaching on the centrality of the church as the *gathered* community in God's purposes for his people and his world. We need this book right now.

Michael Raiter
Director, Centre for Biblical Preaching, Melbourne

Karl has done us a great favour in writing this book. He shows us simply and clearly from the Bible how Jesus loves and cherishes his church, his bride, and why we should love Jesus' church too. As gatherings of Jesus' people, our churches will be communities of joy and love; as gatherings of sinners, they will experience conflict and hurt. All love is costly, but Karl shows us why loving and investing in our church communities will have overwhelming benefits now and in eternity. If you're having trouble being motivated about church, pick up this book. You'll be glad you did. Really!

Al Stewart
National Director, Fellowship of Independent Evangelical Churches (FIEC), Australia

KARL DEENICK

GATHERED TOGETHER

The beauty of living as God's church

matthiasmedia
SYDNEY · YOUNGSTOWN

Matthias Media
(St Matthias Press Ltd ACN 067 558 365)
Email: info@matthiasmedia.com.au
Internet: www.matthiasmedia.com.au
Please visit our website for current postal and telephone contact information.

Matthias Media (USA)
Email: sales@matthiasmedia.com
Internet: www.matthiasmedia.com
Please visit our website for current postal and telephone contact information.

ISBN 978 1 925424 81 2

Cover design by Annesa Fung.
Typesetting by Lankshear Design.

Für meinen lieben Freund Achim.
"Es gibt einen Freund, der anhänglicher ist als ein Bruder."
(Sprüche 18:24)

CONTENTS

INTRODUCTION

Some years ago, a couple of people I know were travelling in a car together when the car started to make a strange sound. One of them suggested they pull into a service station as soon as possible to see if a mechanic could solve the problem. The other person suggested they turn up the radio so they couldn't hear the noise! Thankfully, they chose the former option and had the car looked at. It turned out that another mechanic who had recently worked on the car had made a mistake reassembling the brakes. The results of continuing without fixing the problem could have been disastrous.

The thing about warning signs is that you need to pay attention to them. And for a while now, there have been some warning signs around church life.

Perhaps the biggest warning sign has been the declining number of Christians who go to a church each week. I'm not talking about church attendance across the whole population (although that's a huge issue in itself); I'm talking about people who call themselves Christians and think of themselves as belonging to a church, but simply don't show up from week to week. For example, the numbers in Australia (in a survey taken before COVID) suggest that only 60 to 70 percent of church members attend on any given Sunday.[1] As some have noted, whereas the regulars used to come twice a Sunday, now they come twice a month.[2] Other Christians seem stuck on a merry-go-round of looking for a church, staying at one church for a few years before moving on to another. Similarly, there are a growing number of people who are 'post-church'—they still claim to be Christians, but they've abandoned commitment to any kind of regular gathering with other Christians.

The reasons for this lack of commitment are many: dissatisfaction with what's offered on Sundays; lack of relational connection and meaningful friendships; past hurts from other Christians or churches; busyness that squeezes out the time for church; embarrassment about Christianity's declining social status and fear of what friends and neighbours might think; or disappointment over the church's lack of evangelistic or social impact.

Whatever the reason, it's a major warning sign.

Another warning sign is exhaustion. While many have noted that pastors seem to be burning out more frequently than in generations past, the problem is far broader. Everyone seems to

---

1   M Lean, 'The creeping trend of church absenteeism', *The Gospel Coalition Australia*, 26 April 2017, accessed 1 February 2022 (au.thegospelcoalition.org/article/the-creeping-trend-of-church-absenteeism); see also A Barraclough, 'When did you last go to Church? The spiritual battle it seems like we are losing', *Sydney Anglicans*, 18 September 2019, accessed 1 February 2022 (sydneyanglicans.net/news/when-did-you-last-go-to-church-the-spiritual-battle-it-seems-like-we-are-losing).

2   A Barraclough and D Steele, 'How do you encourage the sheep that God has given you to care for to come to church to hear his word? With Antony Barraclough', *The Pastor's Heart*, 28 August 2018, accessed 1 February 2022 (thepastorsheart.net/podcast/2018/8/28/how-do-you-encourage-the-sheep-that-god-has-given-you-to-care-for-to-come-to-church-to-hear-his-word-with-antony-barraclough).

be exhausted. Sometimes people are exhausted because of church commitments, but often they're simply exhausted from life. Even more problematic is that many feel that church life doesn't seem to help with their exhaustion, but instead makes it worse.

Those warning signs, and the questions they have raised, have become even more prominent during the COVID pandemic and the closure of many churches during the lockdowns. As churches have reopened, many have struggled to coax their members back. Some people have simply dropped off the radar. A recurring theme during COVID was the rest that people found, not just from the busyness of life but also from the busyness of church. In fact, while stopping our public meetings should have been a source of great sadness, for many it was a delightful experience.

Even for me as a pastor, the start of COVID was a kind of little haven. It was in lockdown that I rediscovered the idea of 'personal worship'—an old idea that Christians in past centuries knew. It's not that I'd never spent time in personal devotions. But trapped alone in my house on Sundays, I would spend a couple of hours on my own in Bible reading, personal prayer, singing and lifting my heart up to God. It was such a rich discovery. But why, I wondered, did I not leave our public church gatherings feeling the same way? It almost felt as though it was easier to enjoy God alone at home than it was at church.

Others have rediscovered the joy of meeting with fellow believers in homes, not just to eat and talk about the week, but to sing, read the Bible, hear the Bible taught and pray. They could do that across age groups, with families and with those living on their own. Again, those have been rich experiences. But they've raised questions about things that seem to be missing from our church life.

More than any other question about church, COVID has raised the question of why we gather as Christians at all. Staying at home and watching the sermon online is so convenient. It's easier for the kids. It takes less time. And not only that, but I can also stream the best preachers on the planet right into my lounge room.

This is not to say that good things have not been happening. God has continued to be faithful. But the warning signs have been there for some time. And those warning signs and experiences have raised questions about what church is and what it does. What does it mean to be a church? And by that I mean not "What do *we* think the church is or should be?" but "What does *God* think the church is? What does *God* think the church should be?"

These are important questions not just for a post-COVID world; they're important any time. And they're important not only for pastors, but for every church member. The success and maturity of the church requires far more than church leaders who understand these things. It requires the whole church—every single member—knowing and understanding these things. It is pointless and fruitless for one or two people in a church to understand how God means for his church to live and function if the rest of the church doesn't share this understanding. Because, in the end, it will be the members of the church in whose lives the church will operate.

But the aim of this book is not simply to help you understand the church; the aim is to help you love it.

Despite all the challenges and warnings, I love the church. But that hasn't always been the case. Like any love, it has taken time to grow and mature. And like any love, it's also been tested and tried many times. But by God's grace, over time, I've come to see what a precious thing the church is. I've been blessed by it, and so have many, many others around me. I've written this book because I love the church, and because I want you to love the church. In fact, one of the greatest joys in my life is to see others growing in their love for the church.

Maybe you've never really loved the church. If not, I pray that this book will help you to love it for the first time. I pray you'll come to love it as much as Jesus—the one who gave his life for the church—loves it. Or maybe you already love the church, but you've noticed the warning signs, and you don't know what to do about them. If so, I pray that this book will help you to know how you can keep persevering in loving and strengthening God's church.

This book, then, is a little primer on the church—what it is, what it does, and how it does it. But its perspective is from the pew. It's not a book on how to run a church—there are plenty of those. This is a book to help you live in the church as a faithful member, or, better still, as a faithful partner and co-worker.

1
RESETTING OUR
EXPECTATIONS

Expectations are powerful. They seem to have a disproportionate power to affect our enjoyment of things. Expecting too much can lead to disappointment, while expecting too little can lead us to settle for less than what could or should be.

For example, a couple might enter a marriage with unrealistic expectations of how wonderful married life will be: marriage will solve all their problems, it will cure their loneliness, it will be one moment of joy after another—a perfect partnership. But when reality starts to bite, those unrealistic expectations will inevitably lead to disappointment, bitterness and, at worst, one or both deciding the marriage isn't working and that it would be better for them to separate. On the other hand, another couple might enter marriage with very low expectations. They expect married life together to be full of arguments, and so they settle for a life full of arguments. They expect each other to be selfish, and so they settle for being selfish and don't work to grow in serving each other. They don't expect married life to have any joys, and so they settle for a joyless marriage. Again, those low expectations can lead to one or both deciding that the marriage isn't working and that it would be better for them to separate.

Sadly, the same dynamics often play out in the life of the local church, where many people have wrong expectations. The problem is that sooner or later those expectations take their toll and can lead to bitterness, disappointment and resentment.

In some cases, we can find ourselves expecting our church to be perfect. We would never say it that way, but in practice this is what we expect. So whenever someone hurts us or lets us down, we find it very hard to cope, partly because we didn't expect to be hurt. This unexpected hurt leads many to abandon their church or even abandon the Christian faith altogether. Likewise, we can expect our church to meet all our needs, or we can expect everyone to be our best friends, or we can expect every church meeting to be fabulous and inspiring. Anything less becomes a source of enormous disappointment and discouragement.

On the flip side, we can expect too little. We can assume all our relationships in church will be superficial and casual, and so settle for that, never discovering the delight of deeply loving one another. We can expect church gatherings to always be uninspiring, and so turn up on Sunday with our hearts and minds disengaged. We can expect the church members never to grow or change, and so content ourselves with being stuck in sin.

One of the most important things as we begin our journey of learning to love and live in God's church is to reset our expectations according to the Bible. The church of God is a glorious and wonderful thing that God has called into existence through the gospel, but it's also a place of struggle and sin. And to live in our own church well, we need to hold tightly to both of those truths.

The glory of the church

One of the most common places people turn to think about church is the book of Acts, because it tells the story of the beginning of the New Testament church. Acts begins with the apostles holed up in a room waiting for Jesus to send the Holy Spirit. When the Holy Spirit finally arrives on the day of Pentecost, the age of the Holy-Spirit-empowered New Testament church begins. In a single day, three thousand people are converted. And the result is a brand new, vibrant community of people who are dedicated to hearing the apostles' teaching every day, devoted to prayer, and committed to meeting in each other's homes and generously sharing all that they have.

It's an amazing picture. And as we read on in Acts, it only gets more and more exciting as more and more people are converted. Several times in the early chapters, Luke, the author of Acts, records the spectacular growth of the church at large. For example, "the Lord added to their number daily those who were being saved" (Acts 2:47).[3] The book is full of vibrant spirituality and what seems like daily conversions.

But it's not only Acts that paints a stunning picture of church life. For example, the Bible describes the members of one local church as members of the body of Christ:

> For just as each of us has one body with many members, and these members do not all have the same function, so in Christ we, though many, form one body, and each member belongs to all the others. (Rom 12:4-5)

There is a deep and profound unity not only with each other, but most importantly with God through Jesus. The church in Ephesus

3   See also Acts 2:41, 5:14 and 11:24.

is described as "God's holy people ... the faithful in Christ Jesus" (Eph 1:1). The local church in Corinth was a community of people who had been engaged in all kinds of sinful behaviours but had since been washed, set apart and reconciled to God. The apostle Paul describes their new condition this way:

> Or do you not know that wrongdoers will not inherit the kingdom of God? Do not be deceived: Neither the sexually immoral nor idolaters nor adulterers nor men who have sex with men nor thieves nor the greedy nor drunkards nor slanderers nor swindlers will inherit the kingdom of God. And that is what some of you were. But you were washed, you were sanctified, you were justified in the name of the Lord Jesus Christ and by the Spirit of our God. (1 Cor 6:9-11)

The Corinthian church is also described as God's sacred "temple"—the place where God had chosen to dwell by his Spirit and meet with his people:

> Don't you know that you yourselves are God's temple and that God's Spirit dwells in your midst? If anyone destroys God's temple, God will destroy that person; for God's temple is sacred, and you together are that temple. (1 Cor 3:16-17)

The Thessalonian church was a community of faith, hope and love:

> We always thank God for all of you and continually mention you in our prayers. We remember before our God and Father your work produced by faith, your labour prompted by love, and your endurance inspired by hope in our Lord Jesus Christ. (1 Thess 1:2-3)

It was also a community of eager and powerful witness:

Our gospel came to you not simply with words but also with power, with the Holy Spirit and deep conviction ... you became a model to all the believers in Macedonia and Achaia. The Lord's message rang out from you not only in Macedonia and Achaia—your faith in God has become known everywhere. (1 Thess 1:5, 7-8)

The New Testament vision of church life is extraordinary. The churches are communities of people who were sinners, but who have been justified by the blood of Christ and washed by the Holy Spirit, and who together are now God's dwelling place, God's holy people, God's own treasured possession—people belonging to God. The churches are vibrant communities of ongoing learning of the deep truths of the gospel, communities of rich and constant prayer, of loving relationships, of sharing and generosity. They are communities of faith, hope and love. They are communities that are growing in number. They are communities of gospel power and deep conviction. They are communities of joyful, faithful witness.

We rightly have high hopes for our churches. But the tragedy is that often our hopes are far more mundane than the ones presented in the Bible. Often we hope for lesser things: good music, a short meeting, slick leading, good crèche facilities or a great children's program. And not only do we aspire to those lesser things; we see our failure to achieve those lesser things as an unbearable loss. We're embarrassed by bad PowerPoint slides or dodgy music, while our failure to achieve a community of love, grace, worship and delight in God causes barely a stir.

The first step, then, in living as God's church is to recapture God's vision for the glory of his church. When our hearts are fired by God's vision of the church in the New Testament, our hopes are lifted to much greater things. You could have the worst music in the world, no kids' program or a cold building with no windows and no heating. But if you have a group of sinners saved by grace, indwelt by God, empowered by his grace, filled with love, constant in prayer, overflowing with generosity and labouring in the gospel, then you have everything you could ever hope for or need.

The struggle of the church

Yet God's glorious vision for the church is only one side of the story. If we only consider the kinds of passages listed above, we'll come away with a very distorted picture. The truth is that the Bible presents us with a much more complicated picture of church life.

For instance, while three thousand people are converted in Acts 2 on the day of Pentecost, two chapters later Peter and John are thrown in prison and dragged before the authorities. In Acts 5, Ananias and Sapphira lie to church leaders about giving money and are struck dead by God. In Acts 6, a significant disagreement arises about distribution of the food that's being shared. The church that was supposed to be glorious and united is already suffering and displaying signs of fracturing.

This pattern of incredible success as well as difficult struggle continues throughout the New Testament. In 2 Timothy, Paul says that Timothy's church is full of both true believers and false believers:

> In a large house there are articles not only of gold and silver, but also of wood and clay; some are for special purposes and some for common use. (2 Tim 2:20)

The "large house" that Paul mentions is Timothy's church. In it, there are what Paul calls vessels for "special purposes" and vessels for "common use"—that is, vessels that you use for fine dining and vessels that you use for cleaning the toilet. Timothy's church is a mixture of the good and bad, of the useful and useless, of the clean and unclean. For instance, there are those in Timothy's church who are teaching lies and undermining the faith of others. Their lies are like gangrene—they just keep on spreading, and every time they spread, more of the church dies and more of the church needs to be cut off (2:16-18).

Likewise, Jude wanted to be positive in writing to one particular church, but had to change tack because of the moral and theological problems there. He writes:

> Although I was very eager to write to you about the salvation we share, I felt compelled to write and urge you to contend for the faith that was once for all entrusted to God's holy people. For certain individuals whose condemnation was written about long ago have secretly slipped in among you. They are ungodly people, who pervert the grace of our God into a licence for immorality and deny Jesus Christ our only Sovereign and Lord. (Jude 3-4)

When Paul wrote to the church in Corinth, it was being damaged by favouritism and church politics (1 Cor 1:10-13), sexual immorality (5:1-2), lawsuits (6:1-8), idolatry (10:14-22), and greed and selfishness (11:17-22). The messages to the seven churches in Revelation tell of a church that had lost its love for Christ (Rev 2:4), a church that was engaged in worshipping other gods and in sexual immorality (2:14), a church that was involved in a kind of religious prostitution (2:20), a church that was spiritually dead (3:2), and another that was lukewarm (3:15). The New Testament also tells us about churches that were in danger of deserting the gospel (Galatians 1) or of denying the divinity of Jesus (1 John), or that were pandering to the rich and ignoring the poor (Jas 2:1-13).

One of our greatest mistakes in thinking about our church is that we expect it to be perfect. We read all the wonderful and amazing statements in the New Testament about various churches, but we can forget about all the passages that say difficult things about church life. As a result, we're surprised to find that churches can be difficult; we're surprised to find struggles or sin or weakness. But God has never promised that his church, this side of Jesus' return, will be perfect. The New Testament seems to show that the church will always be mixed and always in danger from corruption.[4] Here on earth, the church is united but divided, holy yet full of sinners, universal but fighting turf wars, faithful but at times heretical.

This is not to say that we should be indifferent to or complacent about sin in the church. Not at all. Paul encouraged Timothy to work hard for the purity of the church. Timothy was to flee sin, patiently instruct his opponents, and have nothing to do with the godless and the immoral who pretended to be Christians (2 Tim 2:16, 22-26; 3:1-5). The reason Paul wrote to Corinth, and the reason Jude wrote his letter, was to encourage those churches—not just the leadership, but every member—to take the purity of their church seriously and to struggle for the purity of their church.

In fact, while the gospel of Jesus Christ is the gospel of peace, the church is the frontline on the battlefield between Christ and the kingdom of Satan. The church is not a haven of peace on earth; it's the frontline in the battle "against the powers of this

---

4   This truth came home to me with great force when I first listened to a talk by Peter Adam: 'Making of a man of God, part 1', *The Gospel Coalition*, 14 March 2009, accessed 1 February 2022 (thegospelcoalition.org/sermon/making-of-a-man-of-god-part-1).

dark world and against the spiritual forces of evil in the heavenly realms" (Eph 6:12).

The church is glorious, and the church will be glorious, but we also need to realize that life in the church this side of eternity will always be a struggle.

Living in the gap

But how do we live rightly in the midst of that struggle? To answer that question, it's helpful to look at one passage where Paul unpacks God's great vision for his church.[5] Paul writes to the church in Ephesus:

> Although I am less than the least of all the Lord's people, this grace was given me: to preach to the Gentiles the boundless riches of Christ, and to make plain to everyone the administration of this mystery, which for ages past was kept hidden in God, who created all things. His intent was that now, through the church, the manifold wisdom of God should be made known to the rulers and authorities in the heavenly realms, according to his eternal purpose that he accomplished in Christ Jesus our Lord. (Eph 3:8-11)

Paul says that God's intent is to make his wisdom known in the heavenly realms. Incredibly, Paul says that God intends to achieve this *through the church*. By saving a people for himself from every tribe and language and people and nation, by reconciling them to himself and to each other and building them into a place in which

---

5   Again, I am indebted to Peter Adam's series of talks. On this point in particular, I found his second talk especially helpful: 'Making of a man of God, part 2', *The Gospel Coalition*, 14 March 2009, accessed 1 February 2022 (thegospel coalition.org/sermon/making-of-a-man-of-god-part-2).

God lives (2:19-22), God is making his glory known to the rulers and authorities in the heavenly places and also to the world through all generations (3:21). The church that Paul has in mind is the church of all believers through all time and in all places.[6] But it has implications for the Ephesians in their own local church. That plan and purpose of God is so wonderful, Paul says, that it should keep the Ephesians from being discouraged by Paul's sufferings: "I ask you, therefore, not to be discouraged because of my sufferings for you, which are your glory" (3:13).[7]

The first way, then, that we live in the midst of the struggle is by remembering God's great intent to make his wisdom known through the church—through gathering together a people for himself.

But the second way that we live in the midst of the struggle is by praying for God's glory to be manifest in the church. Paul continues:

> For this reason I kneel before the Father, from whom every family in heaven and on earth derives its name. I pray that out of his glorious riches he may strengthen you with power through his Spirit in your inner being, so that Christ may dwell in your hearts through faith. And I pray that you, being rooted and established in love, may have power, together with all the Lord's holy people, to grasp how wide and long and high and deep is the love of Christ, and to know this love that surpasses knowledge—that you may be

---

6   We'll think more about the different ways the word 'church' is used in the New Testament in the next chapter.

7   In fact, Paul's sufferings work towards the glory of the Ephesians—his sufferings "are your glory". As he suffers for their sake, the gospel takes root in their lives more and more, and hence they are transformed into the image of Christ "with ever-increasing glory" (2 Cor 3:18).

filled to the measure of all the fullness of God.

Now to him who is able to do immeasurably more than all we ask or imagine, according to his power that is at work within us, to him be glory in the church and in Christ Jesus throughout all generations, for ever and ever! Amen. (Eph 3:14-21)

Paul prays for something we sometimes struggle to see as clearly as we should: that God might be glorified "in the church and in Christ Jesus throughout all generations" (v 21). His vision, then, encompasses both the church across the world and through time, but also, again, the local church in Ephesus which is merely one small part of that bigger "church".

And yet our local churches, as well as the church of God throughout the whole world, so often seem light-years away from the biblical ideal. They are marred by scandals and put down by the media. They are pulled apart by divisions, sometimes over important things like truth, and at other times over unimportant things like what colour the chairs should be. And yet there are moments when we catch glimpses of God's glory in the church. We see it most clearly when the members of a church truly love God and delight in him. We see it when they love each other, share in each other's joys and sorrows, care for each other by generously giving time and money, and prayerfully speak God's truth in love for the building up of one another.

And so what does Paul do? He prays. He gets on his knees and prays for people to be strengthened through the Spirit, that Christ might dwell in their hearts by faith so that "being rooted and established in love" they might be "filled to the measure of all the fullness of God". Nothing short of being filled to the brim with the entirety of God's powerful, gracious, transforming presence will be enough for God's glory to be manifest in the church. And importantly, although God's vision is for his glory to be displayed in the church through "all generations", Paul prays for that big glory project to come about by praying, first of all, for the Ephesians in their local church. Incredibly, the manifestation of God's glory begins in our little local churches.

But what an astonishing prayer to pray! If it wasn't in the Bible, we might not even dare to ask such a thing. And yet I suspect that many of us don't pray that way. We look at the church—either our own or the church at large—and instead of getting on our knees and praying to be completely saturated with the radiant presence of God, we just give up and think that the glory of God in the church is out of reach. Alternatively, we get on with developing our plans to make the church amazing without ever stopping to pray, forgetting that the glory of God in the church takes a miracle of God: the supernatural power of the Spirit and a deep knowledge of the love of God. And yet Paul says that when we pray, God is able "to do immeasurably more than all we ask or imagine".

It's a helpful and revealing exercise to reflect on what you pray or imagine God could do for your church. In fact, many of us probably never (or only rarely) ask God for anything for our churches. And if we do, we only pray for ourselves, our friends or those in particular need.

But if you were to pray for your church, what would you ask God to do?

You might ask God for a church with cutting edge music—or old music, depending on your taste—or a first-class Sunday School and youth program, or a clever new sign that really grabs people's attention, or a website that makes the church seem more vibrant. You might imagine a new foyer, a new backdrop, a new lectern, new chairs or a mini-cafe. But, frankly, if those are the limits of our prayers or our dreams for our church, they are embarrassingly small.

God says his plan is to do so much more through the church than that. God's plan is to make his wisdom known to the rulers and authorities in the heavenly places through the church, by turning sinners into saints, and enemies into friends, and by filling them to the measure of all the fullness of God.

2
WHAT IS
THE CHURCH?

What is the church? If we were to ask around a room of Christians, I suspect we'd find lots of different ideas about what *the* church or *a* church is, or should be. The problem is that often our thoughts on what a church is or should be are set more by subconscious desires or by the culture around us, including the Christian culture, rather than by what the Bible says about the church. But our primary concern is not to understand what *we* think the church should be, but to understand what *God* thinks it should be.

There are lots of things that the Bible says about the church. For example, scholar Paul Minear has counted 96 pictures of the church in the New Testament; these include images like a body, a vine, or the pillar and buttress of truth.[8] While 96 may be a bit

---

8   PS Minear, *Images of the Church in the New Testament*, The New Testament Library, Westminster John Knox Press, 2004.

optimistic, it's clear that the Bible uses lots of different images to draw out aspects of the church.

But although much can be said about the church, there are some central ideas that turn up in numerous parts of the New Testament and which get to the heart of what the church really is. Later in this chapter, we'll look in detail at one passage that pulls together lots of those ideas. But first, it helps to examine what the word 'church' means, before mapping out briefly the overall storyline of the church in the Bible.

What does 'church' mean?

Although the word 'church' for us carries distinctly religious connotations, that was not the case in the first century. Before 'church' was adopted by the early Christians, it was used quite regularly in the ordinary language of Greek-speaking people. By understanding how those Greek-speaking people used the word 'church', we'll come to understand something of why the early Christians adopted that term to describe what they did.

The Greek word that has been translated 'church' in many English Bibles simply refers to an 'assembly' or 'gathering'. In fact, a better English word than church is really 'congregation', because it carries the sense that at the heart of the identity of this group is that it regularly gathers together.[9]

The word 'church' has its roots in Greek democracy. It often referred to an assembly of citizens that met regularly to make

---

9   In fact, William Tyndale's 16th-century translation of the New Testament used the word 'congregation' rather than 'church'.

decisions. In Athens, they met 30-40 times per year.[10] We see the term used in that sense in Acts 19: a crowd in Ephesus gathers in the city theatre, the usual meeting place for the assembly, to deal with the disruption being caused by Paul and his ministry companions. Yet, although the crowd gathers in the appropriate place for the city's meeting, the meeting is not properly constituted. For that reason, the city clerk invites Paul and the others to bring their matters before the proper "legal assembly" on another occasion (Acts 19:39).[11]

But the word 'church' also has connections with the Old Testament. In the ancient Greek translation of the Old Testament, 'church' (*ekklēsia*) is used almost invariably to translate a Hebrew word that also means assembly' (*qāhāl*).[12] Like the Greek political entity, the *qāhāl* derives its primary identity from being together. Theologian Moisés Silva notes that "the term is often used to denote the people of Israel collectively, [especially] when they are viewed in assembly before God".[13]

One of the most important gatherings in the Old Testament is at Mount Sinai in Exodus 19-20, where God gathered the people after delivering them from Egypt. In Deuteronomy 4, Moses reflects back on that experience. He says to the people:

---

10 Silva notes that in the Greek world the 'church' was a "political phenomenon, repeated according to certain rules and within a certain framework. It was the assembly of full citizens, functionally rooted in the constitution of the democracy, i.e., an assembly in which fundamental political and judicial decisions were taken." M Silva (ed), *New International Dictionary of New Testament Theology and Exegesis*, 2nd edn, vol 2, Zondervan, 2014, pp 134-135.

11 See CK Barrett, *A Critical and Exegetical Commentary on the Acts of the Apostles*, vol 2, *Introduction and Commentary on Acts 15-28*, ICC, T&T Clark, 1998, p 931.

12 See Silva, *Dictionary of New Testament Theology and Exegesis*, p 135.

13 Silva, *Dictionary of New Testament Theology and Exegesis*, p 136.

Remember the day you stood before the LORD your God at Horeb [Mount Sinai], when he said to me, "Assemble the people before me to hear my words so that they may learn to revere me as long as they live in the land and may teach them to their children". You came near and stood at the foot of the mountain while it blazed with fire to the very heavens, with black clouds and deep darkness. Then the LORD spoke to you out of the fire. You heard the sound of words but saw no form; there was only a voice. He declared to you his covenant, the Ten Commandments, which he commanded you to follow and then wrote them on two stone tablets. And the LORD directed me at that time to teach you the decrees and laws you are to follow in the land that you are crossing the Jordan to possess. (Deut 4:10-14)

God had instructed Moses to gather the people so that they could hear God's words. That gathering of the whole of Israel before God is called an 'assembly', or, in the Greek version of the Old Testament, a 'church'.[14]

The idea of the church being gathered around God in his presence is picked up again in Hebrews 12, where a comparison is drawn between the Sinai gathering (or 'church') mentioned in Deuteronomy 4 and the gathering (or 'church') of all God's holy people in heaven gathered together right now around the throne of God in Jesus:

You have not come to a mountain that can be touched and that is burning with fire; to darkness, gloom and storm; to a trumpet blast or to such a voice speaking words that those

14 Strictly speaking, the Hebrew uses the verb 'to assemble' (qhl) rather than the noun 'assembly' (qāhāl). Nevertheless, the Septuagint (the Greek translation of the Old Testament) simply uses the noun 'assembly' (ekklēsia).

who heard it begged that no further word be spoken to them, because they could not bear what was commanded: "If even an animal touches the mountain, it must be stoned to death". The sight was so terrifying that Moses said, "I am trembling with fear".

But you have come to Mount Zion, to the city of the living God, the heavenly Jerusalem. You have come to thousands upon thousands of angels in joyful assembly, to the church of the firstborn, whose names are written in heaven. You have come to God, the Judge of all, to the spirits of the righteous made perfect, to Jesus the mediator of a new covenant, and to the sprinkled blood that speaks a better word than the blood of Abel. (Heb 12:18-24)

The writer of Hebrews makes a comparison between God's people gathered in the Old Testament at Sinai and God's people gathered now around Christ in the heavenly places. Whereas the gathering in the presence of God at Sinai was a terrifying and fearful event that threatened death, the gathering of God's people around Jesus is one of joy and celebration. Moreover, according to Hebrews 12, there is a sense in which Christians are already now gathered around the throne of God through the Holy Spirit. The writer does not say "you *will* come", but "you *have* come". You're already there.[15]

Paul says something similar in Ephesians 2:

God, who is rich in mercy, made us alive with Christ even when we were dead in transgressions ... And God raised

---

15 As David Peterson notes, "the vision in 12:22-24 is of the ultimate, completed company of the people of God, membership of which is now enjoyed by faith". D Peterson, *Hebrews and Perfection: An examination of the concept of perfection in the 'Epistle to the Hebrews'*, Society for New Testament Studies Monograph Series (47), Cambridge University Press, 2005, p 162.

us up with Christ and seated us with him in the heavenly realms in Christ Jesus. (Eph 2:4-6)

Believers are already alive with Christ and are already seated with him in the heavenly realms. Wherever you are and wherever you go, if you trust in Jesus, you are gathered permanently with every other believer around the throne of God.

Yet, although that is an incredible idea, there's also something incomplete about it. That is, although we're gathered *spiritually* around the throne of God, we're not yet gathered *physically*. We're scattered all over the world in different countries or different places and even at different times and in different centuries. And so the New Testament says that we're waiting for that physical gathering of all God's people. Paul writes of the moment that our full, physical gathering will finally take place:

> For the Lord himself will come down from heaven, with a loud command, with the voice of the archangel and with the trumpet call of God, and the dead in Christ will rise first. After that, we who are still alive and are left will be caught up together with them in the clouds to meet the Lord in the air. And so we will be with the Lord forever. (1 Thess 4:16-17)

The meeting with Jesus "in the air" does not describe our permanent destination; the term Paul employs could also be used to describe a delegation from a city going to meet a visiting dignitary; the delegation would go out to meet the dignitary before accompanying them back into the city.[16] That helps us to understand what Paul has in mind here. Those who are living when Jesus returns will be taken up into the air to meet with Jesus and with those believers whom he has raised from the dead; together, they

16 See GL Green, *The Letters to the Thessalonians*, PNTC, Eerdmans, 2002, pp 226-228.

will accompany him as he returns to earth to take up his rule and authority over the world.

Revelation, too, pictures this ultimate goal. John sees a new heaven and a new earth, swept free from evil, in which God dwells with his forgiven, restored and renewed people:

> And I heard a loud voice from the throne saying, "Look! God's dwelling place is now among the people, and he will dwell with them. They will be his people, and God himself will be with them and be their God. 'He will wipe every tear from their eyes. There will be no more death' or mourning or crying or pain, for the old order of things has passed away." (Rev 21:3-4)

So there is a *spiritual* heavenly gathering, which is the 'church'. This is often called the 'invisible' or 'heavenly' church. As Christians, we are waiting for that gathering to be fully realized *physically*.

But the New Testament also uses 'church' to describe local, physical gatherings of Christians in particular places. For example, it speaks about "the church of God in Corinth" (1 Cor 1:2) or of believers who "come together as a church" (1 Cor 11:18). As we'll see in more detail later in this book, these are the communities of people who gather regularly with each other in various ways.

Finally, the Bible sometimes uses the word 'church' to talk about Christianity at large. In Acts, Luke speaks about *the* church across a whole range of different regions (Acts 9:31). Clearly the Christians in those areas were not all regularly meeting together.[17]

---

17 There are other passages, too, where the broader earthly church seems to be in view, such as 1 Corinthians 12:28, where Paul says that God has given apostles, prophets, teachers and others to "the church", presumably meaning more than just the Corinthian church. And given that some of the gifts he lists are for this present earthly age, one presumes he doesn't mean the heavenly church.

Sometimes, then, people refer to the church as both 'visible' and 'universal', meaning the worldwide conglomeration of churches.

In some ways, these ideas are all connected. The central identity is, of course, the invisible, heavenly church that the Spirit has already gathered around Jesus. But that heavenly reality is then manifested in the world, primarily in local churches. Nevertheless, it is also, in some way, manifested in the many Christians spread throughout the world in different churches. Importantly, however, because they are on earth, the local church and the worldwide church are imperfect reflections of the spiritual heavenly church. As we saw in the last chapter, they are imperfect because they contain sinners, and they are imperfect because they also contain people who are not truly believers.

The story of the church

Now that we have a basic understanding of what 'church' means, it will also help to know the story of how the church came to be. In a sense, the history of the church only begins in the New Testament on the day of Pentecost, when the Spirit is poured out on the believers gathered in Jerusalem. That great act of God begins the era of the 'church'.[18] Nevertheless, as we've seen, the idea of the church

---

18 Gerald Bray asks whether the Old Testament community of God's people ought to properly be called the 'church'. He writes, "Both ancient Israel and the later Christian church were called 'the people of God,' and if that is what we mean by the word 'church,' then Israel must be included. But the New Testament does not go that far. The differences between the historic institutions of Israel and those of the early Christian movement were just as significant as their similarities, and the way in which Christians used the word 'church' is indicative of that. They recognized that, for all the similarities and connections between them, Christianity was not just a branch of Judaism. If it had been, the disciples of Jesus would never have formed such distinct (and distinctive) worshipping communities. The fact is that although they remained Jews, their spiritual experience could not →

is already floating around in the Old Testament. But although the word 'church' is barely used in the Old Testament, the idea of God gathering a people to himself really begins in the very first chapter of the Bible and lies at the heart of the Bible's storyline.

The story of the church in the Old Testament

God's work of gathering a people to himself began in the garden of Eden. When God created Adam and Eve, he created them to be his people and to live and walk with him in his presence, under his rule and blessing.[19]

Tragically, however, when Adam and Eve rebelled against God's loving rule, they were excluded from God's presence and made subject to death and the other effects of sin. Yet despite that, God offered a promise of restoration. He promised that he would put the world right through a descendant of Eve. God said to the serpent, "I will put enmity between you and the woman, and between your offspring and hers; he will crush your head, and you will strike his heel" (Gen 3:15).

That promise then becomes central to the Bible's unfolding storyline, as the rest of the Bible traces out the search for that single descendant of Eve and records the history of the people who are gathered around that promise. In the very next chapter of

---

be contained within the bounds of traditional Judaism. Furthermore, it was possible (and soon became the norm) for Gentiles to believe in Christ and enjoy the same experience of him without becoming Jews. There was something new here, and it is this that the term 'church' expresses." G Bray, *The Church: A theological and historical account*, Baker Academic, 2016, pp 16-17.

19 For the language of "God's people in God's place under God's rule", see G Goldsworthy, *The Goldsworthy Trilogy*, Paternoster, 2000, pp 53-54, 60. The additional notion of "blessing" comes from V Roberts, *God's Big Picture: Tracing the storyline of the Bible*, 2nd edn, IVP, 2009, p 22.

the Bible, our attention is again drawn to that line of promise.[20] In Genesis 4, after the death of Abel at Cain's hand and while Cain's family line descends further and further into chaos,[21] God provides for Eve "another child" (Gen 4:25) from whom God's promised blessing to the world will come. From there, God raises up Noah. While the rest of humanity will be destroyed on account of their sin, Noah will survive and his family with him. And as with Adam, from that one man will come a renewed humanity. Yet the humanity that comes from Noah is every bit as corrupted as the one that came from Adam.[22]

After Noah comes Abraham. God promises that, through Abraham, blessing will come to the world. In Genesis 12, God speaks to Abraham and says, "Go from your country, your people and your father's household to the land I will show you. I will make you into a great nation, and I will bless you; I will make your name great, and you will be a blessing" (Gen 12:1-2).

Not only will Abraham be blessed, but he will also be a blessing to others. God then reassures Abraham that this blessing will be given to (and through) a son who is Abraham's own flesh and blood (Gen 15:4). That reassurance comes in the form of a covenant—an oath from God that he will certainly do what he has promised (Gen 15:18). Then, in the apparently peculiar sign of circumcision, God enshrines and signifies the promise that through a descendant not only of Eve but now of Abraham too,

---

20 The focus on the line of descendants from Eve is further highlighted in Genesis by the continual focus on one descendant over and above another, such as Isaac rather than Ishmael (Gen 17:19-20) and Jacob rather than Esau (Gen 25:21-26).

21 For example, Cain's descendant, Lamech, boasts about committing murder, proudly claiming that his sin is more nefarious than Cain's (Gen 4:23-24).

22 The doors of the ark have barely been opened when Noah gets drunk and lies naked in his tent, leading one of his sons to take perverse pleasure in seeing his father's naked body (Gen 9:18-27).

God will save a people for himself (Genesis 17).

Although strange to us at first, circumcision signified the promise: that God would raise up a descendant of Abraham through whom he would save a people for himself.[23] Circumcision also served to mark out the community of people gathered around that promise—the people to whom the promise had been made known and whose life and hope were ordered by the hope of that promise. Nevertheless, it was not the sign of circumcision itself that mattered. Circumcision was merely the sign that proclaimed the truth of the gospel—salvation through an heir of Eve and Abraham. What mattered was taking hold by faith of the promise symbolized in circumcision. That heart appropriation of the promise symbolized in circumcision is what the Bible calls "circumcision of the heart" (Rom 2:29; cf. Deut 30:6).

Joining the community that gathered around and trusted God's promise of a descendant of Abraham was possible not only for Abraham's physical descendants, but also for anyone who aligned themselves with what God was doing through Abraham and his promised descendant. Importantly, when promising Abraham that he would be both blessed and a blessing, God had also said, "I will bless those who bless you, and whoever curses you I will curse; and all peoples on earth will be blessed through you" (Gen 12:3). In other words, those who bound themselves to what God was doing through Abraham and his descendant would share the blessing promised to Abraham, while God would reject those who rejected the promise.

This pattern plays out in the rest of Genesis. Insofar as people join up with Abraham (or his descendants Isaac and Jacob) and

---

23 Circumcision was the sign because the promise was about a descendant. Hence the sign was attached to the part of the body responsible for procreation.

what God is doing through him, they are blessed. For example, Laban is blessed by Jacob's presence with him (Gen 30:30), and the Egyptians are blessed by Joseph's presence among them (Gen 41:41-57). Physical blessing through the presence of Abraham's descendants becomes a portent of the spiritual blessing that would come to those who linked up with Abraham's ultimate descendant. Indeed, throughout the rest of the Old Testament, the hope of a single descendant of Abraham (and Eve) through whom God would save a people for himself finds expression in a long line of key figures through whom God gathers, protects and preserves his people—figures like Moses, Joshua, the judges, Samuel, Saul and David.

With the coming of King David, the line of promise is narrowed again. The community of people gathered around Eve's descendant and Abraham's descendant now becomes the community of people gathered around David's descendant. God promises David that one of his descendants will sit on the throne forever (2 Sam 7:12-14). So too, the prophets look forward expectantly to the coming of a descendant of David through whom God will save a people for himself. For instance, God says through Jeremiah:

"The days are coming", declares the LORD, "when I will raise up for David a righteous Branch, a King who will reign wisely and do what is just and right in the land". (Jer 23:5)

Thus, the people of God in the Old Testament were essentially a community of promise—that is, a community gathered around God's promises to Abraham and David. That community was where the gospel, the good news of God's saving work through Abraham's descendant (cf. Gal 3:8), was known and taught. Not everyone within that community was a believer. Some belonged only to the 'visible' community, marked out by circumcision. But others belonged to the 'invisible' community—the *real* community.

Those were the people who took hold of God's promise in their heart and who aligned themselves with what God was doing (and would do) through the promised descendant of Abraham.

The story of the church in the New Testament

It is perhaps unsurprising, then, that Matthew begins his Gospel with a genealogy that traces Jesus' line from Abraham through David and his descendants to Mary and Joseph. He begins by labelling it as "the genealogy of Jesus the Messiah the son of David, the son of Abraham" (Matt 1:1). He then concludes the genealogy by noting that "there were fourteen generations in all from Abraham to David, fourteen from David to the exile to Babylon, and fourteen from the exile to the Messiah" (1:17).

Similarly, Zechariah (the husband of Elizabeth and father of John the Baptist) brings together the promises to Abraham and David in his prophecy about the impending birth of Jesus:

"Praise be to the Lord, the God of Israel,
   because he has come to his people and redeemed them.
He has raised up a horn of salvation for us
   in the house of his servant David
(as he said through his holy prophets of long ago),
salvation from our enemies
   and from the hand of all who hate us—
to show mercy to our ancestors
   and to remember his holy covenant,
   the oath he swore to our father Abraham:
to rescue us from the hand of our enemies,
   and to enable us to serve him without fear
   in holiness and righteousness before him all our days."
(Luke 1:68-75)

The key issue in the New Testament, then, becomes accepting and submitting to Jesus as God's Messiah and King, the promised descendant of Abraham. We see this in Peter's sermon on the day of Pentecost, when he says to the crowd, "Therefore let all Israel be assured of this: God has made this Jesus, whom you crucified, both Lord and Messiah" (Acts 2:36). The necessary response is to repent and be baptized in the name of Jesus (Acts 2:38).

The same concepts are present throughout the New Testament. For example, in Philippians 3 Paul says that the real "circumcision" are those who abandon everything else and take hold of Jesus by faith:

> For it is we who are the circumcision, we who serve God by his Spirit, who boast in Christ Jesus, and who put no confidence in the flesh—though I myself have reasons for such confidence.
>
> If someone else thinks they have reasons to put confidence in the flesh, I have more: circumcised on the eighth day, of the people of Israel, of the tribe of Benjamin, a Hebrew of Hebrews; in regard to the law, a Pharisee; as for zeal, persecuting the church; as for righteousness based on the law, faultless.
>
> But whatever were gains to me I now consider loss for the sake of Christ. (Phil 3:3-7)[24]

It is not Jewishness and the practices of Old Testament Judaism that matter, but rather latching on to Jesus by faith. Indeed, Jesus tells the Pharisees that their failure to receive him and love him means that they are not children of Abraham at all, but children of the devil (John 8:39-47).

---

24 For more on this, see K Deenick, *Righteous by Promise: A biblical theology of circumcision*, NSBT, vol 45, Apollos, 2018, pp 111-130.

In the New Testament, then, the community of God's people (what comes to be known as 'the church') shifts from being a community gathered around a *promised* Messiah to a community gathered around the Messiah *who has now come.* People must put their trust in Jesus as the fulfilment of all God's promises (see 2 Cor 1:20). He is the descendant of Eve, Abraham and David through whom God is saving a people for himself. Belonging to the church requires more than simply believing in God or believing that God exists. It requires more than participating in the ceremonies or practices of a church. It requires more than simply being a member of a local church. As in the Old Testament, there is a kind of 'visible' belonging to a church that doesn't constitute belonging to God's 'invisible' or 'heavenly' church. Belonging to that church requires explicit faith in Jesus as he is revealed in the Scriptures.

A people reconciled to God

With that brief outline of the meaning of 'church' and the story of the church in place, we come to Paul's comments about the identity of the church in one critical passage: Ephesians 2:11-22. Oddly enough, Paul begins this part of his letter by talking about national division:

> Therefore, remember that formerly you who are Gentiles by birth and called "uncircumcised" by those who call them-selves "the circumcision" (which is done in the body by human hands)—remember that at that time you were sepa-rate from Christ, excluded from citizenship in Israel and foreigners to the covenants of the promise, without hope and without God in the world. (vv 11-12)

But Paul is not talking about just any national division; he's talking about the dividing line in the Old Testament between Israel and the rest of the world. The people of Israel were "the circumcision", the ones to whom the promises of God were revealed and entrusted—promises about redemption and about the Messiah. Paul is simply pointing out that if you weren't a citizen in Israel, then you didn't know God's promises about Jesus and therefore you didn't know God and didn't have any hope.

As we've already seen, the boundary between Jews and Gentiles (non-Jews) was not a hard-and-fast dividing line. Non-Israelites could join themselves with Israel and discover God, trust God and love God (think of people like Ruth in the book bearing her name, or Naaman the Syrian in 2 Kings 5:17). But unless someone identified themselves with Israel and with God's promise to Abraham, they were, as Paul says, "without hope and without God". In other words, Paul is saying that every person in the world who didn't know the message God had entrusted to Israel was estranged from God.

You might think, then, that the people of Israel were not estranged from God. But Paul doesn't say that. It turns out that Israel was not in such a great place itself. Paul writes that God's purpose was ...

> ... to create in himself one new humanity out of the two [i.e. Jew and Gentile], thus making peace, and in one body to reconcile both of them to God through the cross, by which he put to death their hostility. He came and preached peace to you who were far away [i.e. the Gentiles] and peace to those who were near [i.e. the Jews]. (vv 15-17)

In other words, both Jews and Gentiles needed to be reconciled to God. The Gentiles were "far away" and needed to be reconciled;

the Jews were "near" and needed to be reconciled.

Paul has already outlined the exact nature of the problem between all human beings and God at the beginning of Ephesians chapter 2:

> As for you, you were dead in your transgressions and sins, in which you used to live when you followed the ways of this world and of the ruler of the kingdom of the air, the spirit who is now at work in those who are disobedient. All of us also lived among them at one time, gratifying the cravings of our flesh and following its desires and thoughts. Like the rest, we were by nature deserving of wrath. (vv 1-3)

The problem is that we are all by nature utterly corrupt—we hate God and are enslaved to Satan. Again, it is both "you" (the non-Jewish Galatians) and "all of us" (Jew and Gentile together) who are in that condition. As a result, we are estranged from God and are objects of his wrath.

So what is God's solution?

God's solution, says Paul, is to reconcile us to himself through Jesus' death on the cross in our place. In Jesus' death, God has put his hostility towards us away—the hostility that resulted from our utter rejection of him. Now those who trust in Jesus "are no longer foreigners and strangers, but fellow citizens with God's people and also members of his household" (v 19).

The language of "citizens" and "members of [God's] household" is nothing less than an Old Testament way of describing the people of God. Paul takes the Old Testament language that was used of God's people and applies it to the New Testament church. It is through Jesus' death that we become part of the people of God. Although faith is the means by which we take hold of what Jesus has accomplished, it is not faith itself that brings us into the heavenly church per se; it is the death of Jesus by which we have been reconciled to God.

So in answer to the question "what is the church?", the most fundamental answer is that *the (heavenly) church is the collection of people reconciled to God through the death of Jesus*. That might seem like a rather obvious point, but it's crucial to remember—not least because it is reflected in the makeup of our local churches. A church is not a group of people committed to working their way to God. It's not a group of people simply trying to live more moral lives. Neither it is a group of people trying to improve the moral condition of society, or who just happen to 'have a lot in common' in some general sense. A church, ideally, is the collection of people already reconciled to God through Jesus. But that also means that a church is *not* a collection of perfect people; a church is, by definition, a group of *sinners* who are reconciled to God because of their trust in Jesus' death on their behalf.

We saw in the last chapter that the church on earth this side of Jesus' return will always be a mixed church—that is, the earthly gathering will contain both true Christians and false Christians. It contains true Christians who flee sin and pursue righteousness as they call out to Jesus and trust in him, and it contains false Christians who are indifferent to sin and who don't call on Jesus but rely on themselves or on something (or someone) other than Jesus. That is, they are people who carry the label 'Christian', who think of themselves as Christians, but who are not really Christians at all. It's tempting to think, then, that if only you could root out all the false Christians then your church would be a haven of rest. But even then, you'd still find that you had an imperfect church, because you'd still have a church full of sinners. What makes a church a church is that it is *a collection of sinners reconciled to God by the death of Jesus*.

A people recreated in Jesus

Yet the church is also more than this. Paul says that being part of the church changes us at the level of our very being: "[God's] purpose was to create in himself one new humanity out of the two, thus making peace" (v 15). Remember that at the beginning of Ephesians 2, the mess we all find ourselves in apart from Christ is total corruption—we hate God and are enslaved to Satan, which means that spiritually speaking we are "dead in [our] transgressions and sins" (vv 1-3). God's solution, then, is not only to reconcile people to himself through Jesus' death, but also to create in Jesus a new humanity.

The Father, through Jesus' life, death and resurrection, has forged in Jesus a new humanity. Jesus entered our world, with all its corruption, and overcame it. He perfected his humanity, transformed it and glorified it (Heb 2:10-12). Moreover, what he did in himself he now shares with others, such that if we entrust ourselves to his loving authority and care, then we participate in that new humanity—Jesus makes us new creations like him. In the language of Ephesians 2, although we were spiritually dead, in Christ we have been raised to life (v 5). Although we were corrupted by sin, we have been created anew in Jesus to do good works in loving service to God (v 10).

This is important because it means that membership of the heavenly church is more than just a matter of ink on paper; it's more than simply having signed on the dotted line. It's more than being committed to a group of people, turning up to the same building once a week, having your name on one of the church rosters, belonging to a small group, having been baptized, or having stood up once and given your testimony. Some of those things are more important than others. But belonging to the church of God, the one gathered around Christ in heaven, is immeasurably more important than any of those things. Belonging to the church of God is something supernatural and spiritual. It is something that God does through his Holy Spirit.

For that reason, belonging to the church is not something that you can do. Rather, *belonging to the church is something you need to ask God to do for you and in you; it is something that God does when you call out to him in faith.* You might attend a local church. You might even feel that you 'belong' to it. But unless you've called out to God by faith and God has made you alive in Christ through his Holy Spirit, then you don't really belong at all, either to the local church or to the assembly of believers gathered around the throne of Christ. You need to ask God to reconcile you to himself through Jesus' death, and you need to ask God to make you a new creation in Christ Jesus.

If you attend a church but have never asked God to do that for you, then stop reading this book and ask God to do that right now. Ask him to make you part of his church through Jesus Christ. Ask him not simply to save you *from* sin, but to save you *into* a living body of sinners who have been reconciled to God through the death and resurrection of Jesus. God says he will not turn away anyone who comes to him through Jesus: "Everyone who calls on the name of the Lord will be saved" (Rom 10:13).

A people united in the family of God

At the heart of the identity of the church are sinners reconciled to God through Jesus and being remade into the image of Jesus through the Spirit. But that has massive implications not only for our relationship with God but also for our relationships with each other. Not only has God set aside the hostility between himself and us, but flowing from that he has set aside the hostility between his people. God has made the two groups—Jew and Gentile—one, and has formed one new humanity so that now our identity in Christ trumps every other identity we have: "through [Jesus] we both have access to the Father by one Spirit. Consequently, you are no longer foreigners and strangers, but fellow citizens with God's people and also members of his household ..." (Eph 2:18-19). We were foreigners, but now we're all citizens together of the same city—God's city, God's new creation in Jesus. We were strangers, but now we're members of God's household, God's family.

Those aren't just labels. As we've seen, it's something that has changed at the very level of our existence. By reconciling us to God through his death, Jesus has opened the way for the Spirit of the living God to come and dwell in us, adopting us into God's family and causing us to be reborn as children of God (Gal 4:6-7). We now share something of God's 'DNA', so to speak, through the Spirit uniting us with the Lord Jesus Christ. Because all believers are all now members of the one family of God, Jesus has abolished the great divisions between Jews and Gentiles. That is what Paul means when he says, "So in Christ Jesus you are all children of God through faith ... There is neither Jew nor Gentile, neither slave nor free, nor is there male and female, for you are all one in Christ Jesus" (Gal 3:26, 28).

The church's identity as the new humanity in Christ, the family of God in Christ, transcends any other identity that we might have, whether age, ethnicity, gender, class, education, interests, favourite sport, or anything else. Theologian Don Carson writes:

Ideally ... the church itself is not made up of natural 'friends'. It is made up of natural enemies. What binds us together is not common education, common race, common income levels, common politics, common nationality, common accents, common jobs, or anything else of that sort. Christians come together, not because they form a natural collection, but because they all have been saved by Jesus Christ and owe him a common allegiance ... they are a band of natural enemies who love one another for Jesus' sake.[25]

The irony is that we often believe this when it comes to the big differences, but we struggle to believe it when it comes to the smaller ones. We love stories like that of Corrie ten Boom, who could forgive and receive the former Nazi concentration camp guard who brutally treated her and her sister.[26] We love the image of those people together in the church—sworn enemies reconciled by Christ. But when it comes to small differences, so often we almost can't overcome them.

This often comes to expression in our local churches. Innumerable times I've spoken with people who've wanted to leave a church or have already left a church because "there's no-one here my age" or "there's no-one here my children's age" or "there's no-one here with the same interests as me". And while those experiences can be genuinely difficult and can push us towards loneliness, we shouldn't allow those to become the main criteria by which we assess the church community. The Bible never encourages us to think of the church as a place where there are lots of people 'like me'. On the contrary, it is characterized as a place where people are 'not like me': Jew, Greek, male, female, slave, free, from every tribe and language and people and nation (Rev 5:9). As Paul says, the church is like a body. There are toes, fingers, noses, ears and hands: they're all different, but each part needs the other. It's not

25 DA Carson, *Love in Hard Places*, Crossway, 2002, p 61.
26 C ten Boom and E and J Sherrill, *The Hiding Place*, 35th anniversary edn, Chosen Books, 2006, pp 247-248.

that you don't belong because you're a nose and everyone else is an eye. You do belong, precisely because you're a nose and nobody else is. Your church doesn't need another eye; it needs a nose. It needs you (1 Cor 12:12-20).[27]

At one level, of course, we understand this. If a missionary said, "I can't be part of this church community because there's no-one here like me, no-one my age, no-one who shares my interests, no-one here my children's age—so I'm going to leave the mission field to find a church where I fit in", we would think they had completely misunderstood their purpose. In the same way, when we say, "I don't belong to this church because people are not like me", we are in danger of failing to understand our purpose and mission as members of Christ's body.

In fact, one of the great privileges and treasures of the church is that in it we have the opportunity to connect with and love people who are not like us. That's what can make church life hard, but it's also what makes it beautiful: we get to relate to all kinds of different people—young and old, male and female, Australian, Chinese, Malaysian, South African, Colombian, or whatever it might be.

A building being built together

But finally, the church is not only something that simply exists and into which we are invited and joined through faith in Jesus. The church is also a building work that is still in progress. Paul says that believers are ...

> ... members of [God's] household, built on the foundation of the apostles and prophets, with Christ Jesus himself as

27 My thanks go to Phil Ninness for making this point particularly clear to me.

the chief cornerstone. In him the whole building is joined together and rises to become a holy temple in the Lord. (Eph 2:19-21)

People often rightly say that the church is not a building, and that's true. St Andrew's Cathedral in Sydney is not the church, nor is the London Metropolitan Tabernacle. The church is the people—the sinners reconciled to God through Jesus.

Nevertheless, Paul says that those sinners reconciled to Jesus are an awful lot like a building. First, they have a cornerstone: a block from which the whole building gets its alignment. That cornerstone is Jesus. Second, they have a foundation: the teaching of the apostles and prophets, which we find written down for us in the Bible. But third, they're also like a building in that they are being built together. As Paul says in the final verse of our key passage, "in [Jesus] you too are being built together to become a dwelling in which God lives by his Spirit" (v 22).

Being "built together" is something that takes place almost intangibly across the whole (heavenly) church throughout time and space. In Christ, through the Spirit, the "whole building" is joined together and is growing. As the Spirit takes the word of God and applies it to our lives, he builds us not only in our relationship with Christ, our head, but also with each other. Miraculously and mysteriously, the Spirit knits us together more closely, day by day, through his word, even with Christians we have never met.

One of the great treasures of the Christian life is to hear missionaries tell stories of people being saved through Jesus; to hear stories of new brothers and sisters throughout the world giving up everything, sometimes literally, to follow Jesus; to pray for these brothers and sisters and send them money as they try to find work or accommodation, having been kicked out by family or friends or employers because they have trusted in Christ; to pray for these new Christians as they risk their lives to share the gospel with others. In doing so, we grow to love them, even if we have never met them.

Nevertheless, what is true of the heavenly church of God scattered throughout the whole world is also true of the local church in Ephesus to which Paul was writing, and it is true of every other local church. Paul says that God is building his "whole" church (v 21), but then adds that "you too" are being built together (v 22). All of God's people are being built together by God's Spirit, but 'you, the Ephesian church, are being built together right where you are'. And, indeed, the reason Paul wrote his letter to the Ephesians was for precisely that purpose: not simply so that the worldwide church could be built up and built together, but so *that particular church in Ephesus* could be built up.

What is largely invisible with respect to the church of God across the world becomes visible in the local church. As part of building together his people across the world, God places us into a local church to grow and be built. That doesn't mean we should separate ourselves off from the world outside or from other churches or from other Christians. But it does mean that our primary place in which God is building us is the local church to which we have committed. As the Ephesians were being built together in their church, so God was building his whole people around the world. As you are being built together in your church, so God is building his worldwide church.

Sadly, many people who claim to be followers of Jesus want to follow Jesus without being part of a church. But a brick on its own is not a building. It's just a brick. In the same way, a person who claims to be a Christian but who doesn't want to be part of a local church cannot really be part of the people of God, because that person is not being built together with the local people of

God. Of course, there are exceptions. For example, there are those who live in countries or towns where there are no churches (or no faithful churches); there are those who can't attend church for physical health or mental health reasons. But in the ordinary course of events, to be a Christian means being built together with others in the context of a local church—a local gathering of believers who are not only committed to God but also committed to each other.

You might find being part of a local church difficult, for many different reasons. For example, you might have deep scars from past hurts you've received in churches. But as painful as those past hurts might be, you really need to ask God to help you deal with those, because God wants you to be part of a local community of believers. In fact, in God's wisdom, it will usually be that community of believers who will help you deal with those hurts. As hard as it can be to face the trauma of bad church experiences, it's so important, because it's not possible to be a Christian on your own. You need to be part of a local church because being a Christian means being built together into a building where God dwells.

So what is the church?

It's the people of God who have been gathered by the Spirit around Jesus in the heavenly places.

It's the collection of sinners reconciled to God through Jesus' death.

It's the collection of reconciled sinners recreated through the work of the Spirit.

It's the collection of recreated sinners united together in the family of God.

And it's the people across the whole world who regularly gather in little outposts of that heavenly church to be built together into the dwelling place of God.

3
WHAT DOES THE
CHURCH DO?

W hen I was an engineer, the company I worked for went through the process of working out its mission and vision statements. From memory, it was a process that stretched over more than a year. When it had finally finished, posters telling us our mission were put up on the walls and in the elevators. I found it mildly humorous, if not downright disturbing, that our senior managers needed to spend a year working out what we were supposed to be doing. After all, the organization by that time had been operating for nearly 50 years.

Although we might think of vision and mission statements as modern phenomena, people have been using them for centuries. They just used to call them 'mottos' rather than mission or vision statements. The school I attended had the motto "All knowledge through Christ", which pretty well sums up what they were trying to achieve. The university where I studied had the motto *Sidere mens eadem mutato*, which, being Latin, kind of lacks the ability to communicate effectively. It apparently means something like "the stars change, the mind remains the same", which, to be honest, doesn't help much either.[28] Even better, the youth group in the church where I grew up formerly had the motto *Pro Rege*, which is Latin for "For the King".[29]

It's tempting to mock mission and vision statements as just another fad of the corporate world, but it's surprising how easy it is to forget your so-called 'core business' and to find yourself doing things that aren't really that important. That can happen in business, but it can also happen in the church. For that reason, it's essential for Christians to know and understand the mission of the church. Why does the church exist? What is its purpose? What should it do?

Thankfully, we don't need to spend a year working out the church's mission, because Jesus himself gave some pretty good summaries to help us know what we're supposed to be doing. In this chapter, we'll focus on the core principles, then in the chapters that follow we'll consider how these principles work out both in the life of the church and in our own personal lives.

Love God

In three of the four Gospels, we find the same story of "one of the teachers of the law" coming to Jesus and asking him, "Of all the commandments, which is the most important?" (Mark 12:28) Jesus replies:

28 The idea is supposed to be something like: "The traditions of the older universities of the Northern Hemisphere are continued here in the South" (sydney.edu.au/heraldry/coat_of_arms/motto.shtml). Again, that pretty well sums up what the university set out to accomplish.
29 Gone are the days when youth groups had Latin mottos!

"The most important one ... is this: 'Hear, O Israel: The Lord our God, the Lord is one. Love the Lord your God with all your heart and with all your soul and with all your mind and with all your strength.'" (Mark 12:29-30)[30]

The most important thing that any person should be doing is loving God with all their heart, soul, mind and strength. And if that is the most important task for any person, then it is certainly the most important task for the church as well.

When God first formed his great community of saved people in the Old Testament, having brought them out of Egypt, he said to them, "you will be for me a kingdom of priests and a holy nation" (Exod 19:6). In the Old Testament, the priests were the people who God set apart to serve him. Their whole lives were to be lived out in the presence of God, in and around the temple, and devoted to the service of God. Similarly, to be 'holy' means to be 'set apart' for God's special purpose. But in Exodus 19, God says that the whole nation was to be like that. They were *all* to be set apart for God; they were *all* to be devoted to the service of God. In other words, their great purpose in being saved was to live before God and for God.

How were they to do that? The answer to that question comes in Exodus 20, where God gives them the Ten Commandments. The Ten Commandments are really ten dot points—a summary of the shape of life in God's community under God's rule and provision. Yet Jesus summarizes the Ten Commandments even further into two key commands. The first of these is to love God with all our being.

The great goal of the church, then, is to do that—to love God with all our heart, soul, mind and strength. All the activities that

30 See also Matthew 22:34-40 and Luke 10:25-28.

a church does ought to be geared towards that end. It ought to be the key reason for gathering on Sunday and in small groups during the week. It ought to be the reason we pray, study the Bible, read Christian books and organize church lunches. The aim in everything is to grow in our love for the Father, Son and Holy Spirit. A church that does that will be a place of deep, profound and life-giving joy. It will be a place of delight and sustenance.

But as with any good mission statement, it's good to keep going back to it and asking the question: Is that what we're doing? Are we loving God? Are our Sunday gatherings about loving God and growing in love for God? Are our small groups aimed at that? Are our evangelistic efforts?

It's worth taking a moment to reflect on that. But it's also worth taking a moment to reflect on whether those are the criteria you normally use to evaluate how your church is going. Too often we evaluate our church on other grounds, like how well we think the church is doing in loving *us* or loving *our* children, or the quality of the kids' program or the music, or how far we have to drive to get there. Yet if the chief criteria by which we evaluate a church is how well it is loving *us*, then we're putting ourselves in the place of God himself. If the chief criterion by which you evaluate your church is how well it fits in with your kids' life, then you're making your children your god. If the chief criterion by which you evaluate your church is the music, then you're making music your god. If the chief criterion by which you evaluate your church is how long it takes to get there, then you're making convenience your god.

Instead, we need to ask: Is our church a place where people love God with all their heart, soul, mind and strength? Is delight in God at the centre of everything we do? Are we constantly re-ordering our lives to do the things that delight God? Am I doing that? Are the people around me doing that? Are my children doing that? A church will never do that perfectly, of course. But is that our aim? And when we fail to do that as a church, do we confess that to God and seek his forgiveness and grace?

When a young man falls in love with a woman, she can often become the centre of his life and of everything he does. He thinks about her all the time. He wants to spend all his time with her. He wants to do everything he can to please and delight her. That's how God is asking us to relate to him. God wants to be at the centre of everything we do and think. When he disappears from the centre, the church dies. But when the church remains focused on loving God, it can thrive.

Love our neighbours

But having given the most important commandment, Jesus also adds a second part to his answer: "The second [commandment] is this: 'Love your neighbour as yourself'. There is no commandment greater than these" (Mark 12:31). In Luke's account of this conversation, the religious leader follows up with another question: "And who is my neighbour?" (Luke 10:29). Jesus responds with the story of the 'Good Samaritan':

> "A man was going down from Jerusalem to Jericho, when he was attacked by robbers. They stripped him of his clothes, beat him and went away, leaving him half dead. A priest happened to be going down the same road, and when he saw the man, he passed by on the other side. So too, a Levite, when he came to the place and saw him, passed by on the other side. But a Samaritan, as he travelled, came where the man was; and when he saw him, he took pity on him.

He went to him and bandaged his wounds, pouring on oil and wine. Then he put the man on his own donkey, brought him to an inn and took care of him. The next day he took out two denarii and gave them to the innkeeper. 'Look after him', he said, 'and when I return, I will reimburse you for any extra expense you may have'.

"Which of these three do you think was a neighbour to the man who fell into the hands of robbers?"

The expert in the law replied, "The one who had mercy on him."

Jesus told him, "Go and do likewise." (Luke 10:30-37)

The shocking answer of Jesus' parable is that the Jewish man's neighbour is his despised enemy, a Samaritan. Jesus says something similar in the Sermon on the Mount:

"You have heard that it was said, 'Love your neighbour and hate your enemy.' But I tell you, love your enemies and pray for those who persecute you, that you may be children of your Father in heaven. He causes his sun to rise on the evil and the good, and sends rain on the righteous and the unrighteous." (Matt 5:43-45)

Jesus says we are to love our enemies. In fact, Jesus calls us to be like God in this way. God loves his people with a special love, but God also sends rain on both the righteous and the unrighteous and causes the sun to rise on the evil and the good.[31] In the same way, the church ought to be a community of people who imitate the love of God, not just for our friends, but also for our enemies.

As Christians, we ought to be genuinely and deeply concerned

---

31 For some of the different ways the Bible speaks about the love of God, see DA Carson, *The Difficult Doctrine of the Love of God*, Crossway, 2000, pp 16-21.

for those around us. We ought to give generously, share what we have, listen to others, weep with others, show deep compassion, and care for the poor and helpless. We ought to show such love not only to those who are nice to us, but even to those who hate us.

That might mean helping a work colleague who is constantly undermining you. It might mean helping your neighbour who is at war with you. It might mean giving a lift to someone with whom you don't really get on. In doing these things, we fulfil an important part of the mission of the church.

Nevertheless, the most important way that we can love our neighbours is by urging them to be reconciled to God through Jesus (2 Cor 5:20). It is hardly loving to feed someone but fail to give them the message that will save them from everlasting damnation.[32] Again, we ought to show such love not only to our friends but also to our enemies.

In that light, while the idea of 'friendship evangelism' can be helpful, we also need to be careful to recognize that Jesus calls us to more; he calls us love people who are our enemies, and the way we love them most of all is by calling them to come and know him. For that reason, perhaps a more helpful idea than 'friendship evangelism' is 'love evangelism'—that is, telling people the gospel in the context of showing love rather than only in the context of friendship. Why the distinction? Primarily because you don't

---

32 In the words of the atheist and magician Penn Jillette, "If you believe that there's a heaven and a hell, and people could be going to hell or not getting eternal life, and you think that it's not really worth telling them this because it would make it socially awkward ... how much do you have to hate somebody to *not* proselytize? How much do you have to hate somebody to believe everlasting life is possible and not tell them that?" Quoted in J Taylor, 'How much do you have to hate somebody to *not* proselytize?', *The Gospel Coalition*, 18 November 2009, accessed 1 February 2022 (thegospelcoalition.org/blogs/justin-taylor/how-much-do-you-have-to-hate-somebody-to-not-proselytize).

have to be friends with someone to love them by sharing the gospel with them. After all, Jesus says we ought to love people who aren't our friends; we ought to love our enemies.

Yet it is important to realize that loving our neighbours is not simply a means to an end. We don't simply love people so that we can share the gospel with them. We love people because God commands us to do it, but more importantly because in loving people we reflect our heavenly Father, who also loves them and gives generously to them. That is, we don't love our neighbours in order that we might have an opportunity to 'do mission' (i.e. evangelism). Rather, just as in loving God we are fulfilling the most important part of the mission of the church, so too in loving our neighbours we are fulfilling one key part of the mission of the church.

Love the church

But there's another way in which the New Testament applies the command to love our neighbours. Not only is it applied to our enemies; it is also applied to the church itself. For instance, Paul writes to the Colossian church:

> Therefore, as God's chosen people, holy and dearly loved, clothe yourselves with compassion, kindness, humility, gentleness and patience. Bear with each other and forgive one another if any of you has a grievance against someone. Forgive as the Lord forgave you. And over all these virtues put on love, which binds them all together in perfect unity. (Col 3:12-14)

Paul calls the church to love each other deeply. Their love is to be marked by compassion, kindness, humility and patience. They are to forgive rather than harbour grudges.

That command to love our brothers and sisters in Christ is scattered throughout the New Testament. Jesus commands his disciples to love one another:

> "A new command I give you: Love one another. As I have loved you, so you must love one another. By this everyone will know that you are my disciples, if you love one another." (John 13:34-35)

"One another" implies their mutual love for each other as fellow believers. That is not to say they ought not to love the world around them too. Rather, it is to suggest that their special love for one another is what will particularly mark them out.[33]

Similarly, according to 1 John, one of the great tests of whether we really belong to Christ is whether we love our fellow Christians:

> We know that we have passed from death to life, because we love each other. Anyone who does not love remains in death. (3:14)

> Everyone who believes that Jesus is the Christ is born of God, and everyone who loves the father loves his child as well. (5:1)

There is evidently a *priority*, too, with respect to love for God's people. Paul writes in Galatians, "as we have opportunity, let us do good to all people, especially to those who belong to the family of believers" (Gal 6:10). In other words, one of the special ways that love for our neighbours is worked out is through love for the church. That doesn't mean that we love people in the church to

33 DA Carson, *The Gospel According to John*, PNTC, Eerdmans, 1991, p 485.

the exclusion of those outside. But it does mean that loving the church has primary importance.

At one level, that's fairly obvious. Of course we should love those in the church more, because the church is the body of Christ; we're family. Our fellow church members are the ones in whom the Spirit of God lives. But at another level, you might think it's a bit strange. After all, surely loving people outside the church is a much harder thing to do. Surely loving people in the church is a bit of a cop-out.

But that's not always the case. Sometimes the most difficult people to love are those who are closest to us. The more time we spend together, the more likely it is that issues will arise that expose our own sin, or theirs. So too, the deeper the love we have for someone, the more costly it is. We're often much more hurt by the betrayal of those closest to us than we are by those we hardly know.

This holds true within the church. It's much harder to love Christians whom you see every week in your local church than it is to love a Christian on the other side of the world whose missionary newsletter you read. That's because the person you see every week is more likely to get on your nerves or say or do something hurtful. When that happens, we're often deeply wounded by it. While we can accept a measure of rejection by society at large, rejection and betrayal by people in our local church can be devastating.

For example, you might give yourself to serve others in your church through some ministry, only to have someone come and unload on you because they didn't like what you did. Or you might invest a great deal of time in loving and discipling some-one, only for them to tell you they're leaving the church because no-one cares about them. Or you might come to church faithfully week after week and try to get to know people, but they ignore you. Or maybe everyone is very polite, but no-one ever invites you into their home or accepts the invitation to visit your home.

To continue to love people and give yourself to them despite these kinds of disappointments is immensely costly. But that's exactly what God calls us to do. It cost Jesus his life to love the church. If it cost Jesus his life, why would we think it would cost us any less?

Make disciples

The two 'Great Commandments' map out for us the task of God's people: love God with all our being, and love our neighbours as ourselves, especially in the church but also in the world. But aside from those two Great Commandments, there is another element that is rightly identified as a key part of what the church does. It's what is referred to as the 'Great Commission'.

After Jesus' resurrection, the eleven disciples go to Galilee where Jesus meets them and gives them this charge:

> "All authority in heaven and on earth has been given to me. Therefore go and make disciples of all nations, baptizing them in the name of the Father and of the Son and of the Holy Spirit, and teaching them to observe all that I have commanded you. And surely I am with you always, to the very end of the age." (Matt 28:18-20)

Jesus gives those first eleven disciples, and through them all disciples, the task of making more disciples from every nation. This task is twofold. First, it involves bringing people to know God through the proclamation of the gospel—calling people to repentance from sin and faith in Jesus. Second, it involves growing people to maturity through the proclamation of the gospel.

People are lost and on their way to an eternity without God, under the judgement of God. As Christians, we have the good news that they can be spared from that judgement if only they turn from sin and entrust themselves to Jesus. Not only as individual Christians, but as churches, as communities of people gathered together around Jesus, we have the responsibility to make that message known.

But the task does not end once a person comes to faith in Jesus. We must continue to teach and instruct them, Jesus says, to obey everything he has commanded. God's goal for us is maturity in Christ. And the Great Commission calls us as Christians and as churches to work towards that end. As Colin Marshall and Tony Payne demonstrate in their book *The Vine Project*, our aim is to engage, evangelize, establish and equip people through the gospel.[34]

Rescued and transformed

Domain of darkness
engage » evangelize »

Kingdom of the Son
» establish » equip

A redeemed people gathered around the risen Christ

The diagram shows that a key part of our role as churches is to *engage with* and *evangelize* those who don't know God. As we do that, by God's grace, some will receive the gospel by faith and be brought into the kingdom of God. But our task does not finish

---

34 C Marshall and T Payne, *The Vine Project: Shaping your ministry culture around disciple-making*, Matthias Media, 2016, p 147. Diagram reproduced with permission.

there. We must continue to bring them to maturity in Christ by *establishing* them in the faith and *equipping* them to serve God and to serve one another.

The task of the church is to love God with all our heart, soul, mind and strength; to love the church; and to love our neighbours. But it's also to make disciples of all nations. It is to speak to people about what God has done in Jesus, and to plead with them to turn from sin and trust and follow Christ. It is to teach people to obey everything that Jesus has commanded us.

So how do the Great Commandments and the Great Commission fit together?

First, the *goal* of the Great Commission is to win more people to loving, adoring and serving God in Jesus. In other words, *the great goal of the Great Commission is the fulfilment of the Great Commandments*.

Long after everything else has passed away, long after the need for mission has ended when Jesus returns, long after the task of the church in taking the gospel to the nations has ended, we will still be loving God with all our heart and loving each other as ourselves. As John Piper has written:

> Missions is not the ultimate goal of the church. Worship is. Missions exists because worship doesn't. Worship is ultimate, not missions, because God is ultimate, not man. When this age is over, and the countless millions of the redeemed fall on their faces before the throne of God, missions will be no more. It is a temporary necessity. But worship abides forever.[35]

---

35 J Piper, *Let the Nations Be Glad! The supremacy of God in missions*, 3rd edn, Baker Academic, 2010, p 35.

Nevertheless, for the moment there is an urgent priority to the Great Commission, because people must hear the gospel if they are to come to know and love God and love each other. People must hear us explain to them that they are sinners under the judgement of God, that they are God's enemies in need of forgiveness through Jesus' death, and that they must turn from their sin and trust in Jesus. Unless they hear that message, they can't be saved.

It is sometimes said: "Preach the gospel; use words if necessary".[36] But that completely misunderstands the nature of the gospel. The gospel is, by definition, a message. It is the proclamation of what God has done in Jesus.[37] Moreover, actions without explanation are likely to be misunderstood. When Jesus performed miracles, people often misunderstood his purpose until he explained it to them (e.g. John 6). So too, without words people will mistake the purpose of our good deeds. They might, for instance, misunderstand our good works as an attempt at works-based righteousness—the idea that we earn a good standing before God by what we do. Similarly, without words people will inevitably see areas of hypocrisy in even our best good deeds and so fail to understand that our hope lies ultimately not in ourselves but completely in Christ and what he has done for us.

Loving people is not evangelism. Loving people is our responsibility before God, and God will hold us to account for that. But people will not mysteriously absorb the gospel through us being nice to them. They'll absorb the gospel through us *speaking* to

---

36 Those words are popularly attributed to St Francis of Assisi, but are not his words at all. See M Galli, 'Speak the gospel: use deeds when necessary', *Christianity Today*, 21 May 2009, accessed 1 February 2022 (christianitytoday.com/ct/2009/mayweb-only/120-42.0.html).

37 See DA Carson, 'What is the gospel?—revisited', in S Storms and J Taylor (eds), *For the Fame of God's Name: Essays in honor of John Piper*, Crossway, 2010, p 158.

them and *teaching* them about God, sin, and salvation in Jesus.[38]

But there's another connection between the Great Commission and the Great Commandments. Not only are the Commandments the *goal* of the Commission; *the Great Commandments are also part of the foundation for the Great Commission.* If we truly love God with all our heart and soul and mind and strength, then we will be desperate for people to know him and be reconciled to him through turning from sin and trusting in Jesus. We'll be desperate for people everywhere to honour God as he deserves. And if we truly love others, we won't be content to remain silent about eternal judgement. Instead, we'll love them by speaking the uncomfortable truth to them so that they may be saved. We'll do that even to our enemies. We'll tell them with tears in our eyes that they are sinners in need of salvation, but that God is a God who welcomes humble and repentant sinners.

In other words, the Great Commission is the meat in the sandwich of the Great Commandments. The Great Commandments are both the foundation and the goal of the Great Commission. Our love for God and for our neighbours will drive us to make God's grace in Jesus known to our neighbours, in order that, having received that grace, they too might grow to maturity in loving God and loving their neighbours.

What is the mission of the church? *The mission of the church is to love God with all our heart, soul, mind and strength, to love the church, to love our neighbours, and to bring others to know and love God by going and making Jesus known.*

---

38 As Tim Keller has noted, we must distinguish between the gospel message itself and the results of the gospel. The gospel is the good news of what God has done in Jesus, but that gospel message transforms those who receive it to be people who love God and others. See TJ Keller, *Center Church: Doing balanced, gospel-centered ministry in your city*, Zondervan, 2012, pp 30-31, 36-37.

4
THE CHURCH GATHERED

If you've been a churchgoer for many years, you'll probably have developed the habit of heading off to church every Sunday to meet God's people and publicly declare the praises of God. But why do you do that? Why do any of us do that? Is it really important?

In a way that very few things have ever done, COVID has raised the question of why we gather as Christians. That question was probably already floating around before the pandemic, but COVID has brought it to our attention in a unique way. For months, many Christians around the world couldn't gather (as I write, some countries are still facing significant restrictions). While at first this came as a bit of a shock, if we're honest some of us found it a kind of pleasant relief. It was so easy not to go to church. It was so peaceful to be able to take your time, sit at home, and engage with the sermon when and how you wanted.

That experience has raised many questions about the church. Why do we make the effort to get out of our pyjamas and drive all the way to church to meet every week? Can't we achieve the same things in other ways? Why do we do that when, if we stay at home, we can listen to the sermon in our own time without the distractions of people getting up and down or walking past the windows? Why do we gather at church with others when at home we can have a lovely time together as a family? Why do we gather when the kids find it easier to play with toys on the floor at home, or when we could just wait until they're in bed before we put the sermon on, or when we don't have to stress about the kids playing up? Why do we gather when, for those of us who are introverts, it's simply easier not to? Can't we have our peace and quiet while still engaging meaningfully with God and being fed by his word?

Gathering is what the church is

In chapter 2, we saw that gathering lies at the heart of the very definition of the word 'church'. It also lies at the heart of the storyline of the Bible: God is gathering a people by the Spirit around his Son, Jesus. Believers are already gathered *spiritually* around the throne of Christ in heaven, and one day we will be gathered *physically* by Christ when he returns to judge the living and the dead. This means that gathering is not just something that Christians have randomly ended up doing. On the contrary, gathering is one of the most foundational aspects of the church. And just as the people of God gathered in the Old Testament era, the people of God also gather in the New Testament era.

Importantly, though, the model of gathering has changed in the move between the Old and New Testaments. In the Old Testament, the community that gathered around the promised Messiah was a single community under one central leadership, led by one man (people like Moses, Joshua, the judges and King

David), whose rule anticipated the rule of that promised Messiah. In the New Testament, the church is gathered around the Messiah, Jesus. But instead of being one single community under one leadership, the church throughout the world consists of many churches or communities, each gathered around Jesus as the "great Shepherd" (Heb 13:20), the "Chief Shepherd" (1 Pet 5:4) and "Overseer" (1 Pet 2:25), with "shepherds" or "elders" acting as local leaders within those communities (1 Pet 5:1-4). So, rather than all the people of God gathering together in one place as in the Old Testament, the New Testament presents a pattern of local believers gathering together regularly in smaller groups. These local gatherings are now the backbone of the life of the heavenly church on earth. And, as we've seen, they are the place where we are built together into one building (Eph 2:22).

As we wait for the final physical gathering of all God's people when Jesus returns, God has called us to gather physically in the local church. Those local gathering are reflections of the present *spiritual* reality in which believers are gathered around the throne of Christ, but they are also anticipations of a future *physical* reality in which Christ will come to gather his people once and for all.[39] In these local churches, a group of sinners—reconciled to God through Jesus' death, recreated through the work of the Spirit, and united together in the family of God—live out on a small scale an invisible cosmic reality.

Every week when you gather in your local church, whether it's large or small by worldly standards, you enact that invisible reality. By being there together every week under the lordship of Jesus, rich and poor, young and old, Australian and Malaysian

39 P Jensen, 'What is church for?', *The Briefing*, 13 December 2011, accessed 1 February 2022 (thebriefing.com.au/2011/12/what-is-church-for).

or whatever your ethnicity, you manifest God's glory in gathering a people to himself who are being built together into a holy temple. Just being there every week with each other has cosmic significance.

The church is defined by its gathering

But that's not all. Gathering every week with God's people not only has cosmic significance; it also changes and shapes our identity. We saw in chapter 2 that the word 'church' has its background in both the Greek political assembly and the Old Testament gathering at Mount Sinai. But what is remarkable about the Greek political assembly, the Old Testament assembly and the New Testament church is that in each case *the gathering helps to define the identity of the people, not the other way around.*

In the Old Testament, the actual gathering of the people before God at Sinai was something that only happened at that one moment in time, but their identity as God's people—gathered together before him to hear his word—was not something that only existed in the moment they were together. It was an identity they took with them into their everyday lives.

The same is even more true of the New Testament church. As we've already seen, the church is a collection of people being built into a building—into the temple of God:

> Consequently, you are no longer foreigners and strangers, but fellow citizens with God's people and also members of his household, built on the foundation of the apostles and prophets, with Christ Jesus himself as the chief cornerstone. In him the whole building is joined together and rises to become a holy temple in the Lord. (Eph 2:19-21)

The sails of the Sydney Opera House are made up of over one million tiles. If you stand up close to the Opera House, the tiles look quite ordinary. One or two tiles, or even ten or twenty tiles, don't look particularly spectacular. But if you stand right back and see what they make up together, you'll find yourself looking at one of the greatest works of architecture the world has ever seen. You don't look at the Sydney Opera House and think, "Wow, what a great collection of tiles!" You think, "Wow, what a great building!" The tiles get their identity from the building, not the other way around. If you remove a tile from the building—if you take a crowbar and prise away a tile, steal it and hang it in your room—the tile loses its significance. It won't have the same glory in your room that it had as part of the whole building. Moreover, whatever glory it does have as it hangs in your room comes not from the tile itself, but from the fact that it was once part of the famous, glorious building.

Although it is deeply countercultural and even possibly offensive to some, the same can be said of the church—not simply the church of God gathered in heaven, but also the local church. Our significance and identity come from being part of the body of Christ. Of course, the most important aspect of this is our connection with Christ himself, who is the head of the body (Col 1:18). But by being connected with Christ, we are automatically and unavoidably connected with his people.

We tend to think of ourselves as a collection of individuals who each have a relationship with Jesus, and who just so happen to be in the same place at the same time every week. But the biblical view is the opposite: we are a gathering of people—a church—and we then take that communal identity into our individual lives.[40] Yes, our identity is ultimately defined by Christ. But Christ is the cornerstone of a *building*. And Christ is the head of a *body*. As extraordinary as it sounds, our identity as Christians, then, is profoundly connected to our regular, local gathering.

Not only is this true theologically; it's also true practically. Our life together in our local church shapes us. That's the whole point of it. The activities we do together—like hearing God's words from the Bible, praying together and caring for each other— shape us and transform us, more and more, into the image of Christ (Col 1:28). Moreover, we are not simply being built up as individuals, but as Paul says, we are being built *together*.

Theologically and practically, your identity as a Christian is shaped by the local church gathering in which you meet regularly. If COVID has raised many important questions about church, I suspect at least part of the reason is simply that our individualistic society had already destroyed our biblical conception of the church.

Gathering from house to house

But what about the mechanics and practicalities of those gatherings. How do we gather? What do we do when we gather?

The New Testament seems to present two main ways in which the early Christians gathered: publicly, and from house to house. We see this even in the ministry of Jesus, who taught in synagogues (Luke 4:16-28), on mountains (Matt 5:1-2), to large crowds (Mark 6:34), and from a boat (Matt 13:1-2). But he also

---

40 As Chris Slater writes, "The phenomena the gospel initiates is [sic] more than the coincidence of people in one place. It's the calling of strangers into family—and the ability of the family unit to thrive is directly proportionate to the quality of relationships that exist within it." C Slater, 'Poles apart', in A Mitchell (ed), *FAQs: Biblical answers to youth and children's leaders questions*, The Good Book Company, 2006, p 117.

GATHERED TOGETHER

taught in homes and to small numbers: he taught his disciples in a private house (Mark 7:17); he taught in a Pharisee's house (Luke 7:36), in Zacchaeus' house (Luke 19:5), and in Mary and Martha's house (Luke 10:38-42).

We see a similar pattern in Acts, where Luke tells us that, after the first day of the New Testament church, "every day [the believers] continued to meet together in the temple courts. They broke bread in their homes and ate together with glad and sincere hearts ..." (Acts 2:46). A similar picture is painted just a few chapters later: "Day after day, in the temple courts and from house to house, they never stopped teaching and proclaiming the good news that Jesus is the Messiah" (5:42). Likewise, Paul tells the Ephesian elders that he taught "publicly and from house to house" (20:20).

Throughout Acts, we see people meeting in each other's homes in organic and sporadic ways. For example, Cornelius gathered a small group of relatives and friends to hear Peter (10:24). Having escaped prison, Peter went to the house of Mary, the mother of John, where people had gathered to pray for him (12:12). Paul ministered in Lydia's house (16:15) and the Philippian jailer's house (16:34). After being thrown out of the synagogue in Corinth, the Christians met in the house of Titius Justus (18:7). In Troas, Paul raised Eutychus from the dead after he fell out of the third-storey window of someone's house, having fallen asleep while Paul was teaching (20:7-12). Paul later stayed and ministered in the house of Philip the evangelist (21:8). Throughout the whole book, there is an energy and devotion to meeting informally and frequently with each other in homes, for fellowship, but especially for teaching and prayer.

In a similar way, many churches today run a network of small groups (which generally go by names like 'Bible study groups', 'growth groups', 'connect groups', or some similar variation). These small groups of house-to-house meetings are a place for relational connection that is often not possible to the same extent in larger weekly gatherings. Indeed, for some people, over time, these groups become like little families.

That's certainly true of my small group. It's a very mixed bunch: we have married couples, people with kids and without kids, and people in their 20s through to people in their 50s. Some members of the group have been together for several years, while others have been part of the group for less than one year. But we've become like a little family. We love each other, do things together and look out for each other, and every week we're growing in loving each other more and more deeply.

But growth groups are not the only way that we can meet from house to house. During COVID, many Christians seem to have rediscovered the rich benefits of organic house-to-house meetings with other Christians. Not only that, but they've also discovered the joy of meeting with a spiritual agenda. In the past, we might have had people over for lunch or dinner, but we didn't sing together or pray together. But the reality of small groups of people meeting in each other's homes to watch livestreamed services created a situation where people were meeting with a clear spiritual agenda, and where people are now growing more and more comfortable doing that.

In fact, what is precious, and what the New Testament models for us, is not simply hospitality but *spiritual* hospitality—that is, meeting together in each other's homes not just for food, but for the explicit purpose of being built up in the faith through fellowship over the word and prayer. Sure, it's great to meet house to house and have fun, watch movies and play board games; but it's rich beyond imagining to be able to engage spiritually with God's people around God's word.

Gathering as the whole church

But, as we noted above, the early church not only met house to house; they also met together publicly. The pattern of temple preaching in Acts 2 soon grew to include other kinds of public gatherings, such as in synagogues (13:5), the lecture hall of Tyrannus (19:9), a recognized place of prayer (16:13), large crowds (11:26), and even a whole city (13:44).

Significantly, the language of 'church' seems to be reserved for these larger gatherings that incorporate the *whole* church. While it's true that as Christians we gather in all kinds of different ways and at different times, not all of those gatherings are rightly called 'church'. In 1 Corinthians, Paul uses the idea of being 'in church' or of the whole church 'coming together':

> In the first place, I hear that *when you come together as a church*, there are divisions among you, and to some extent I believe it. (11:18)

> So then, *when you come together [as one]*, it is not the Lord's Supper you eat ... (11:20)[41]

> But *in the church* I would rather speak five intelligible words to instruct others than ten thousand words in a tongue. (14:19)

> So *if the whole church comes together* and everyone speaks in tongues, and inquirers or unbelievers come in, will they not say that you are out of your mind? (14:23)

---

41 The Greek contains a phrase that the NIV leaves untranslated (*epi to auto*), which means something like "in the same place" or "as one". The same expression occurs throughout the early chapters of Acts to describe the meetings of the early Christians (Acts 1:15, 2:1, 2:44).

For Paul, those four expressions are roughly equivalent:

come together as church = come together as one = in church = whole church comes together[42]

Significantly, the "whole church" that Paul has in mind is not the whole of the church as it existed in the world in the middle of the first century AD, nor is it even the whole of the church in the Mediterranean region at the time. It is the whole of the Corinthian church to whom Paul was writing.[43]

This means that there is an activity called 'church' that involves not just a subset of the body, but the whole body. It involves all the members of the church coming together.[44] It is when the whole of the local church meets together that it anticipates in the fullest sense the gathering of believers around the throne of Christ in

42 They are roughly equivalent not only in that they use the same terminology ("gather", "church", "whole" and "as one", the fullest example being 1 Corinthians 14:23, where "the whole church comes together [as one]"), but also in that the structure of the sentences in both 11:18-20 and 14:19-23 links the expressions *within* each chapter, while the structure of the argument through chapters 11-14 links the expressions *across* the chapters.

43 There is some debate about whether the whole of the Corinthian church could meet together in one place. The issue is whether there was any place large enough to accommodate them. The evidence from 1 Corinthians 11 and 14 seems to suggest that Paul expected that they could meet. So too, in 1 Corinthians 5, Paul anticipates the whole church coming together to exercise discipline against the man caught in adultery. Moreover, if Paul wrote Romans from Corinth (which is very likely; see DA Carson and DJ Moo, *An Introduction to the New Testament*, 2nd edn, IVP, 2005, pp 393-394), then in Romans 16 he refers to the "whole church" being accommodated by Gaius (16:23). Significantly, Romans 16:23 uses the same language to refer to the "whole church" as in 1 Corinthians 11 and 14. Similarly, the first two chapters of Acts show that there, at least, a group of 120 people could meet in one house (1:15 and 2:1-2; cf. DG Peterson, *The Acts of the Apostles*, PNTC, Eerdmans, 2009, p 132). There is no reason to suppose that the same could not have been possible for the church in Corinth.

44 As Silva puts it, "[church] has the nature of an event", hence "coming together must be reckoned an essential element in the [church] (cf. 1 Cor 11:18)". Silva, *Dictionary of New Testament Theology and Exegesis*, p 139.

heaven. In that sense, the church is not simply a 'community' or a 'network', since neither of those terms finds its primary identity in gathering. Nor is the church simply a 'set' of people who may or may not happen to bump into each other from time to time. Instead, *the (local) church is a group of people who meet regularly, all together, to be built up to maturity in Christ.*

Think about a family gathering. For a family gathering to be a family gathering, it requires the whole family (more or less) to be there. It's not a family gathering just because a few family members are there; you can't just meet with your dad and call it a 'family gathering'. Sure, one or two people can be missing and it can still be a genuine family gathering. But if the whole family is never together all at once, or if one or two people are always missing, it starts to have an effect.

In the same way, the gathering of the church requires the *whole* church.

Of course, the larger the family, the harder it is to get everyone together—people can't make it for one reason or another, even when they want to. That's even more true of church. So it's tempting to want to ask, "How many can be missing before it ceases to be a 'family gathering'?" But in asking that question, we begin to lose sight of the point: the purpose of a family gathering is to gather the *whole* family together! The same is true of the church.

This also makes sense of the New Testament's building imagery. We can't be built together with the rest of the building unless we're seeing them and meeting with them regularly. You can only be *built together* by *being together*. It's hard to build a building with some of the bits missing—any kid who has played with Lego will tell you that (as will anyone who's tried to assemble flat-pack furniture!).

This has implications for how we think about our public gatherings when the whole church comes together. It means that the ideal is for the whole church or congregation to meet together.[45] Sure, that will almost never be possible, because somebody will be sick or on holidays. That's fine. But the point is that being built together requires a high frequency of the whole church meeting together. Our disposition ought to be towards being all together as much as possible. And just as a family gathering without someone present always leaves us a little sad, so should church without someone present—even if they're absent for a good reason. As mentioned in the introduction, the current trend in Australian churches of only 60 to 70 percent of a congregation being together on a typical Sunday shows that many people have failed to grasp the nature of the church at this point.

It also means that during COVID, when congregations were unable to meet altogether, the church, in the strict sense, was not meeting. This is not to say that nothing good was done or that no-one grew during this time; it is simply to point out what seems a rather obvious point: we were seriously limited in being able to grow together into one body. In fact, this also answers the question that COVID has raised about why we bother to gather when we can "just do livestreamed church at home": because 'livestreamed church' is not quite 'church' after all.

This also has important implications for how we think about house-to-house gatherings of Christians. For instance, you might gather in your home with other Christians, as many did throughout

---

45 Many churches in Australia have multiple 'congregations' in the one 'church'. The question often arises how we should understand those dynamics. The question is further complicated by the fact that 'church' and 'congregation' are both suitable translations for the underlying Greek term. My own view is that we ought to see the 'congregation' as the primary place of belonging and effectively as the actual 'church' to which people belong. This is because a church is formed not by calling it a 'church' but by the practice of a fixed group of people regularly meeting together to be built up to maturity in Christ.

the pandemic. You might meet with other Christians from other churches. In some of these gatherings, you might do lots of things that you normally do at church, like read the Bible, pray, sing, and hold each other accountable. These gatherings might even be semi-regular or very regular. Undoubtedly such gatherings can be and often are incredibly rich and wonderful experiences. But are they church? The answer that the New Testament gives is no. 'Church' is when the whole 'church' meets—the whole local body; the whole local family.

What does the church do when it gathers?

But what does the church do when it gathers? In Acts 2, when the New Testament church first begins to gather, we can observe several activities that clearly are central to their life together. Luke writes:

> They devoted themselves to the apostles' teaching and to fellowship, to the breaking of bread and to prayer. Everyone was filled with awe at the many wonders and signs performed by the apostles. All the believers were together and had everything in common. They sold property and possessions to give to anyone who had need. Every day they continued to meet together in the temple courts. They broke bread in their homes and ate together with glad and sincere hearts, praising God and enjoying the favour of all the people. And the Lord added to their number daily those who were being saved. (Acts 2:42-47)

They devoted themselves to hearing the apostles teach about Christ. They also met together to pray, something that is at the heart of what the church does throughout the New Testament:

not just one or two people praying from the front, but the whole church joining in prayer. The church also shared generously with each other.[46] They praised God, no doubt through song, but also through simple words of praise and adoration. They devoted themselves to fellowship and to the breaking of bread—probably not a reference to sharing the Lord's Supper, but simply to eating together.[47] Although it doesn't seem very spiritual, eating together is such a wonderful thing to do because, apart from the gospel, food is about the only other thing that we have in common. Eating together can be incredibly significant for forming relationships.

As you read through the rest of Acts and the New Testament, you find these same aspects repeated, along with some other aspects of meeting together. For example, God's people gathered to speak intelligible words that would convict unbelievers:

> If the whole church comes together and everyone speaks in tongues, and inquirers or unbelievers come in, will they not say that you are out of your mind? But if an unbeliever or an inquirer comes in while everyone is prophesying, they are convicted of sin and are brought under judgement by all, as the secrets of their hearts are laid bare. So they will fall down and worship God, exclaiming, "God is really among you!" (1 Cor 14:23-25)

46 What Acts describes in Acts 2:44 is not 'communism', where no personal property ownership exists. Rather, Luke tells us what it means for them to have "everything in common" in his very next sentence: "They sold property and possessions to give to anyone who had need" (Acts 2:45). In other words, as needs arose, the Christians did whatever was required to meet those needs.

47 The expression 'breaking bread' occurs several times in the New Testament, sometimes to refer to the Lord's Supper (Matt 26:26; Mark 14:22; Luke 22:19; 1 Cor 10:16, 11:24), but often simply to refer to the ordinary act of eating together (Matt 14:19, 15:36; Mark 6:41, 8:6; Luke 9:16, 24:30; Acts 20:7, 11; 27:35). In New Testament times, breaking the bread was simply a standard part of sharing out the food among those present.

They gathered to speak or sing words that would edify and build up:

> When you come together, each of you has a hymn, or a word of instruction, a revelation, a tongue or an interpretation. Everything must be done so that the church may be built up. (1 Cor 14:26)

They gathered to teach, admonish and sing:

> Let the message of Christ dwell among you richly as you teach and admonish one another with all wisdom through psalms, hymns, and songs from the Spirit, singing to God with gratitude in your hearts. (Col 3:16)

They gathered to worship, or literally to offer themselves in humble service to God,[48] to fast, to pray and to send missionaries:

> While they were worshiping the Lord and fasting, the Holy Spirit said, "Set apart for me Barnabas and Saul for the work to which I have called them". So after they had fasted and prayed, they placed their hands on them and sent them off. (Acts 13:2-3)[49]

---

48 As Marshall notes, "worshipping means serving God, and is a Greek word originally used of doing public service at one's own expense and then applied in the Greek Old Testament to the cultic service of the priests and Levites in the temple" (IH Marshall, *Acts: An introduction and commentary*, TNTC, vol 5, IVP Academic, 2008, p 229).

49 These verses only explicitly mention the prophets and teachers. However, the mention of the church in verse 1 as the context for the prophets and teachers, together with the fact that the whole church gathers to hear the report of Paul and Barnabas when they return (Acts 14:26-27), suggests that the whole church is involved in sending them—much as the church is involved in appointing the seven men to serve the widows (6:2-6) and those sent out to report on the decision of the Jerusalem council (15:22). See J Stott, *The Message of Acts: To the ends of the earth*, BST, 2nd edn, IVP, 2006, pp 216-217.

They gathered to hear reports from the missionaries they had sent:

> On arriving there, they gathered the church together and reported all that God had done through them and how he had opened a door of faith to the Gentiles. (Acts 14:27)

They gathered to hear the report of the theological dispute that was settled at the Jerusalem council and to encourage and strengthen the believers:

> They gathered the church together and delivered the letter. The people read it and were glad for its encouraging message. Judas and Silas, who themselves were prophets, said much to encourage and strengthen the believers. (Acts 15:30-32)

They gathered to exercise church discipline:

> So when you are assembled and I am with you in spirit, and the power of our Lord Jesus is present, hand this man over to Satan for the destruction of the flesh, so that his spirit may be saved on the day of the Lord. (1 Cor 5:4-5)

They gathered to celebrate the Lord's Supper—or, rather, what should have been the Lord's Supper:

> When you come together, it is not the Lord's Supper you eat ... (1 Cor 11:20)

There are also numerous commands to the churches that, while not explicitly restricted to the church's gathering, presumably form a key part of its gathered life as well. For example, Christians are to encourage each other to resist sin and persevere in faith:

> But encourage one another daily, as long as it is called "Today", so that none of you may be hardened by sin's deceitfulness. (Heb 3:13)

They are to love and serve one another:

> Above all, love each other deeply, because love covers over a multitude of sins. Offer hospitality to one another without grumbling. Each of you should use whatever gift you have received to serve others, as faithful stewards of God's grace in its various forms. (1 Pet 4:8-10)

Clearly, then, there are a variety of different elements of what the church does when it gathers. But perhaps we can summarize it like this: the church gathers to hear the message of the gospel, to encourage one another with the gospel, to make the gospel known to unbelievers in their midst, to pray to God on the basis of the gospel, to praise God for the gospel, to hear about the work of the gospel, to send people into gospel ministry, to remember the gospel in the Lord's Supper (and baptism), to love and serve each other on the basis of the gospel, and to apply the gospel to sin in the church.

The aim of all this is to bring people to maturity in the gospel of Jesus Christ. As Paul writes to the Colossians, "[Christ] is the one we proclaim, admonishing and teaching everyone with all wisdom, so that we may present everyone fully mature in Christ" (Col 1:28).

What God calls the church to do when it gathers is stunningly simple. It isn't rocket science. The trick, however, is to believe God when he says this is what he wants us to do, then to do it with perseverance, believing that God will bless us through it.

Very often we want to invent new things to do and new ways of doing them. Whether that's special ceremonies, meaningful rituals or exciting additions, we pursue these innovations in the hope that they'll empower our spiritual lives. Yet in doing so, we fail to believe God when he tells us we don't need all that; we simply need to hear God's words about Jesus, believe them, pray out of them, praise God because of the truth of them, apply them to our lives, apply them to the church, apply them to sin, declare them clearly to those who are not believers, constantly bring them to mind, and celebrate them. God says that is all we need to be mature Christians and a mature church.

The dangers of not gathering

So far, we've considered the positive reasons for gathering. It's important because it has cosmic significance, because belonging to a local church defines and shapes who we are as Christians, and because it trains and equips us to live the Christian life in all kinds of ways. But before we finish, it's important to consider the dangers that arise when we don't gather. The book of Hebrews warns us about exactly that:

> And let us consider how we may spur one another on toward love and good deeds, not giving up meeting together, as some are in the habit of doing, but encouraging one another— and all the more as you see the Day approaching. [For] If we deliberately keep on sinning after we have received the knowledge of the truth, no sacrifice for sins is left, but only a fearful expectation of judgement and of raging fire that will consume the enemies of God. (Heb 10:24-27)

The encouragement here to keep meeting together is linked with the warning about deliberate sin that follows.[50] One of the most important reasons that we ought to meet together regularly is so that we will not be hardened in sin. The warning is not so much

50 In the original Greek, verse 26 is connected to verse 25 by "for".

that people will completely give up the faith and become atheists, although that is certainly one of the dangers we face. Rather, the warning is that if we are not meeting together, sin will slowly take hold of our lives. The danger is that we might still claim to be following Jesus, but our profession of Christian faith becomes a sham, and our life, marked by ongoing deliberate sin, tramples Jesus underfoot.

Gathering together with other Christians is a protection against being hardened by the sin that lives within us. We need people around us who will keep reminding us of the truth of the gospel and of God's claim on our lives. We need people who know us well enough to be able to challenge us in our sin. We also need the shepherds of the church, whom God has placed over us, looking out for us and warning us. Gathering with God's people challenges our selfishness and pushes us to love other Christians instead of simply being content with loving ourselves. Moreover, it strengthens our doubting hearts, which need to be constantly reminded to hope in Christ. A friend of mine used to say to people floating from one church to the next, "If you're not part of a church, in three years you won't be a Christian". It seems like an extraordinary thing to say, but that's the kind of warning God gives us in Hebrews.

The pattern of people becoming hardened in sin before ultimately giving up the gospel is so tiringly familiar. I've seen it so often. What happens is that people just gradually stop turning up. Sometimes it's simply because life gets too busy. But inevitably, over time, the result is that their commitment to following Jesus diminishes. They swear it won't, but it does. The writer of Hebrews speaks of this as *drifting away* (2:1). Like sitting in an untethered boat, you're not deliberately moving anywhere, but over time you just drift and leave Christ behind.

Other times, people move away from meeting because of conflict. They think to themselves, "I can't forgive that person; I have to leave the church". But over time, they simply become hardened in dangerous bitterness and unforgiveness. Sometimes it happens because a person feels left out, so they decide to conduct a kind of experiment: "Will anyone notice if I leave?" Instead of talking about their loneliness, they secretly put everyone else to the test. They silently walk away and wait to see if anyone comes chasing after them. Without fail, they discover (they think) that no-one loves them, and they become hardened in resentment. Still others leave because they think they're not getting anything out of coming to church. They withdraw, failing to realize that one of the things they were getting out of it was the constant challenge to believe the gospel and to turn away from sin. Sooner or later, then, their lives become plagued by sin and eventually they give up on the gospel altogether.

Time and again, people's first inclination is to withdraw from church. But it's about the worst thing that you can do. It's not that missing one week of church will harden you into unbelief, nor does it mean that there will never be reason to stay away. Rather, the danger lies in the pattern of withdrawal and in a low estimation of how God's power is working out through the church, irrespective of how you feel about it.

Why is it important to go to church? Shockingly, here's the answer that Hebrews gives: so you don't go to hell. Not because church makes us right with God; Jesus' death and resurrection do that. But the church is God's instrument to keep us from turning away from Jesus.

Fundamental to the notion of the church and the people of God is gathering. Gathering to praise God, to hear God's good news about Jesus, to apply God's words to our lives, to pray, to be brought to maturity in Christ and built together into the dwelling place of God, and to ensure that we stay the course without drifting away from God or being hardened by sin's deceitfulness.

5
THE CHURCH
SCATTERED

You might never have thought about it, but most of our life is not lived in our Sunday gatherings or in small groups or in youth group or in meetings with other Christians. The amount of time would vary widely for different people, but I suspect that for many of us it probably boils down to no more than four hours a week in church activities. That's remarkable when you consider that there are about 112 waking hours in the week. Church takes up about three percent of our time—and even that's only if we attend on Sunday *and* we're part a small group during the week.

So although gathering in church (as well as house-to-house gatherings) is central to our Christian lives, we also need to think carefully about what we do with the 97 percent of our time when we're scattered throughout all the places God has put us. How do we fulfil the Great Commandments and the Great Commission when we're scattered in homes, streets, suburbs, families, workplaces, community groups and wherever else we might be?

The church scatters

The New Testament letter of 1 Peter provides crucial insights into the nature of the scattered church. The letter begins with Peter speaking about this exact reality: "Peter, an apostle of Jesus Christ, To God's elect, exiles *scattered* throughout the provinces of Pontus, Galatia, Cappadocia, Asia and Bithynia" (1 Pet 1:1).

Peter was writing to Christians scattered throughout the known world. The Greek word he uses refers to what is known as the 'diaspora', a word used to describe the Jews in the Old Testament who had been *dispersed* throughout the world as a result of their defeat at the hands of the Babylonians and the Assyrians. By some estimates, in Peter's day only one million Jews were living in what was formerly the land of Israel, while somewhere in the range of two to four million were living outside of it.[51]

Yet, strange as it may seem, one of the results of God's judgement on the people of Israel was that the message of God went out beyond Israel. For example, Luke tells us that on the day of Pentecost there were God-fearing Jews and converts to Judaism from every nation under heaven (Acts 2:5-11). The reason there were converts to Judaism from many nations was, in part, because through God's judgement his people had been scattered to all those places.

Later in Acts, we again see the unexpected positive effects of God's people being scattered, although this time not because of judgement, but because of persecution:

> A great persecution broke out against the church in Jerusalem, and all except the apostles were scattered throughout Judea and Samaria. ... Those who had been scattered preached the word wherever they went. (Acts 8:1, 4)

51 PH Davids, *The First Epistle of Peter*, NICNT, Eerdmans, 1990, p 46.

Quite remarkably, the Bible's pattern is that the scattering of God's people throughout the world actually leads to the gathering of God's people.[52] As Christopher Ash notes, the church in this age is paradoxically a "scattered gathering".[53] Similarly, Dietrich Bonhoeffer writes:

> Until then [the end of this age], God's people remain scattered, held together in Jesus Christ alone, having become one because they remember *him* in the distant lands, spread out among the unbelievers. Thus in the period between the death of Christ and the day of judgement, when Christians are allowed to live here in visible community with other Christians, we have merely a gracious anticipation of the end time.[54]

The scattering of the church builds the church. By being scattered throughout the world, God's people take the gospel to schools, building sites, sports clubs, community bands, office buildings, shopping centres, skate parks, jails, craft groups, community gardens, other towns, other states and other countries. The gospel reaches many parts of the world not because a church decides to run an activity there, but because individual Christians plug themselves into those areas of society.[55]

---

52 Another example of this dynamic is seen in Egypt. In the later chapters of Genesis, Joseph's persecution by his brothers led him to bring God's mercy to Egypt. Later, during the exodus, many Egyptians left with the people of God, choosing to go with them rather than to stay with their own people (Exod 12:38).

53 C Ash, *Remaking a Broken World*, rev edn, The Good Book Company, 2019, p 164.

54 D Bonhoeffer, *Life Together and Prayerbook of the Bible: Dietrich Bonhoeffer Works*, vol 5, GB Kelly (ed), Fortress Press, 1996, p 28 (emphasis original).

55 Importantly, the church is not an enclave. It is not a community of people who live together and cut themselves off from those around them. A comparison with an early Jewish sect from the same time as the New Testament is revealing. The so-called Qumran community, to whom the Dead Sea Scrolls belonged, lived in a gated community with shared possessions and no personal property →

In fact, the great diversity of people in churches that makes it hard for us to gather—because we're so different, which causes conflicts and challenges—is the very same diversity that makes the church an incredibly strategic enterprise. You can take the gospel to places that I could never take the gospel, and I can take the gospel to places where you could never take the gospel. This is all part of the wonderful plan and purpose of God.

This is important because we're often tempted to make church the place where Christians must do most of their serving. Pastors can unwittingly pile up church activities and expect people to serve in their mini-kingdoms, failing to realize that God has placed people in other important places where they can serve. Similarly, church members themselves can often equate participation with having a 'job' to do in the church.

One of the great discoveries of the Reformation was the "priesthood of all believers": the idea that ministry is not left to the 'professionals', but that every Christian serves God wherever they are. Yet in recent decades the "priesthood of all believers" has become the "priesthood of all believers on Sunday". That is, we often try to squeeze everyone's Christian service into an hour or two on one day of the week; we jam-pack the Sunday gathering with as many contributors as possible, because we implicitly believe that service on Sunday is what counts, even though when challenged we might say we don't really believe that.[56]

[cont] ownership. The community itself was the place of sanctity. The church, however, is not like that. Instead, the (local) church is a group of people who meet together regularly to be built up to maturity in Christ but who then disperse to go about their distinct lives in the situations where God has placed them.

56 In the past, at least, one of the reasons that pastors existed was because Christians recognized there was value in setting aside a person to serve the church full-time so that others could serve God in their busy lives.

A member of my church once apologized for not being able to serve in more ways in the church. This was a man who was working in a form of chaplaincy where he was constantly sharing the gospel. It was a job that placed high demands on his time and emotions, meaning that he was not able, at the time, to commit to much more. While I appreciated his apology, I also wanted him to know that the ministry in which he was engaged every day of the week was far more important and was having a much greater impact than if he served on one of our church ministry teams. God had put him in that situation, and that was his primary task. My hope was that he could come to church on Sundays after a difficult and draining week to be recharged, so that he could go out again in the coming week to serve God and other people with renewed energy. But my hope was not only that he could be recharged himself, but that he could also take our gathering on Sunday as an opportunity to help recharge others in small but meaningful ways as he spoke the truth of the gospel to people, prayed with them and encouraged them.

Another function of failing to recognize the scattering dynamic of the church is that every idea becomes an idea for the *whole* church. Imagine you have an idea for an exciting gospel initiative, but then you try and co-opt the whole church into it. Maybe all your friends like wine and cheese, so you suggest the church run an evangelistic wine-and-cheese night, not realizing that most people's friends aren't really into that. Or perhaps you have young children, so you think the best way to evangelize is through the whole church getting on board with a holiday kids' club, not realizing that the rest of the church is made up of ex-criminals who would struggle to pass their police checks.

The scattering of the church means that we don't need to make the church do everything *we* want to do. As Kevin DeYoung and

Greg Gilbert write:

> Don't make a church program for every good deed Christians might do in Christ's name. If you have a church member who really wants to see better playground equipment at the downtown park, you could take this on as a church, or you could encourage this brother to spearhead this with families in his neighborhood. It might even make a good outreach opportunity, and it might save your people from ministry overload and from feeling guilty about not doing everything.[57]

The New Testament offers a surprisingly lightweight model for church life: it doesn't seem to have run a great multitude of church programs; rather, it gathered together for people to be built up by the gospel in order to then scatter and take that gospel with them into their daily lives.

Winning disciples

But how does that happen? How is God building his church through the scattering of his people? The rest of 1 Peter goes on to give us the broad outlines of an answer. Peter's entire letter is about equipping God's people to live for God's glory as exiles, scattered throughout the world. Look how Peter describes God's people:

> But you are a chosen people, a royal priesthood, a holy nation, God's special possession, that you may declare the praises of him who called you out of darkness into his wonderful light. (1 Pet 2:9)

---

57 K DeYoung and G Gilbert, *What Is the Mission of the Church? Making sense of social justice, shalom, and the Great Commission*, Crossway, 2011, pp 258-259.

As we noted earlier, the priests in the Old Testament were the people who served God. Their whole lives and work were carried out before God and for God. The work involved both offering up praise and worship to God and declaring the knowledge and praises of God among the people.

We are to live holy lives, serving God wherever we are. But a key part of that is to "declare the praises" of God. Wherever we are, the praise of God ought to be on our lips. That, however, is not merely an act of private worship; it is an act of public evangelism. We not only declare the truth of God's greatness *to* him, but we declare the truth *about* God *to* others. Evangelism is fundamentally an act of praise. We speak about God because we're excited about God. As one keen evangelist in my church puts it, "Evangelism is the greatest act of worship". If we're not speaking about God to unbelievers, it often means that our love for God has grown cold.

But we not only speak the gospel; we also live out the implications of the gospel. Peter continues:

Dear friends, I urge you, as foreigners and exiles, to abstain from sinful desires, which wage war against your soul. Live such good lives among the pagans that, though they accuse you of doing wrong, they may see your good deeds and glorify God on the day he visits us. (1 Pet 2:11-12)

As strangers in the world, we're to live out the gospel of righteousness through Jesus Christ. We are to live our lives "among the pagans", scattered throughout the world, living in such a way that it bears witness to the greatness and the glory of God—the aim being that those who do not know God might ultimately come to faith and so end up glorifying God on the day when Christ returns to gather his people.[58]

How do we do that? Peter gives us some concrete examples. First, he says, we're to submit to the authorities: "Submit yourselves for the Lord's sake to every human authority" (1 Pet 2:13). Diligent and careful obedience to governments, councils, the police, government agencies and even frustrating regulations are a witness to the world of our freedom in Christ—our freedom in Christ to obey, rather than our slavery to sin in which we used to be trapped.

Second, while remembering that ancient slavery is not the same as our modern workplaces, there is instruction here for how we're to live in our working relationships: "Slaves, in reverent fear of God submit yourselves to your masters, not only to those who are good and considerate, but also to those who are harsh" (1 Pet 2:18; cf. Eph 6:5-9; Col 4:1). Our behaviour in the workplace, both as employers and employees, is a witness.

Third, we're to live well in our relationships at home:

Wives, in the same way submit yourselves to your own husbands so that, if any of them do not believe the word, they may be won over without words by the behaviour of their wives, when they see the purity and reverence of your lives. (1 Pet 3:1-2)

Husbands, in the same way be considerate as you live with your wives, and treat them with respect as the weaker partner and as heirs with you of the gracious gift of life, so that nothing will hinder your prayers. (1 Pet 3:7)

---

58 Peter gives a similar example of an unbeliever "seeing" good deeds and then coming to faith in 1 Peter 3:1-2 when he says that the behaviour of believing wives might win their husbands to faith "when they see the purity and reverence of your lives". See WA Grudem, *1 Peter: An introduction and commentary*, TNTC, vol 17, IVP, 2009, p 124.

As Paul says in Ephesians, the way husbands and wives live ought to reflect the gospel. Husbands ought to give themselves up for their wives as Christ gave himself up for the church; they ought to exercise costly love. And wives ought to submit to their husbands, as the church submits to Christ. They ought to model respect and trust in Christ (Eph 5:22-33).

One of the most significant ways in which Peter calls these Christians to live as witnesses is by suffering. The theme of suffering is found right at the beginning of the letter, where the exiles' suffering is purifying them so that their lives will result in "praise, glory and honour when Jesus Christ is revealed" (1 Pet 1:7). The same theme takes up most of chapter 3 and all of chapter 4 in Peter's letter: we are to suffer as Christ suffered (4:1); we are to suffer for doing good (3:17); we are to rejoice in sufferings (4:13). It's striking to think that such an important part of the way we live for God scattered throughout the world is by suffering. I can't help but wonder if, perhaps, the reason our evangelism in the West seems so muted is because of our reluctance to suffer.

Moreover, in all these actions, the goal is not simply to be moral or 'good'. Rather, the goal is to live lives that are radically and comprehensively shaped by the gospel that we believe and by the God to whom we have become slaves (2:16). All these activities are anchored in the gospel. We live them out as we come to Jesus, the "living Stone" (2:4), as we "crave pure spiritual milk" (2:2), as people who have "received mercy" (2:10), and as those who have been born again "into a living hope through the resurrection of Jesus Christ from the dead" (1:3). These are not just moral criteria lived out in a vacuum; they flow out of trust in and love for God through Jesus Christ. As such, they say something about the gospel—about our freedom in Christ, the sufferings of Christ, the love of Christ, and our obedience to Christ.

Nevertheless, the ultimate hope is that we might have an opportunity to speak.

> But in your hearts revere Christ as Lord. Always be prepared to give an answer to everyone who asks you to give the reason for the hope that you have. But do this with gentleness and respect ... (3:15)

The hope is that we'll win an opportunity to speak words about who Jesus is and what he's done. After all, words must be spoken for the gospel to go out. As Paul asks, "How can they believe in the one of whom they have not heard? And how can they hear without someone preaching to them?" (Rom 10:14) The hope is that our lives, saturated with the power of the gospel of Jesus Christ, will win a hearing for the message about Jesus Christ. We ought to be praying for those opportunities, and praying that when they come we will take them with great boldness and confidence in God.

Peter's point is that our fulfilment of the Great Commission is lived out in the context of our ordinary lives. It's not fulfilled mostly on Sundays or even in our church-organized activities. Of course, it should be done there, too. The gathered church is a witness to the gospel in its preaching, singing, praying, and love for God and one another.[59] So too, it is vital for the members of the church to partner together to help one another make disciples. Very few of us, if any, can win and train disciples entirely on our own without the help of our brothers and sisters in Christ. The point is not that we don't make disciples when we gather. We do. The point is that the percentages matter. Most of our disciple-making takes place in our everyday context and relationships.

---

59 For helpful thoughts on this, see J Dickson, *The Best Kept Secret of Christian Mission: Promoting the gospel with more than our lips*, Zondervan, 2010, chapter 10 ('Heralds together: promoting the gospel through our public praise').

Training disciples

The scattered church, however, is not only built up by the addition of new Christians; it's also built up by the strengthening of existing Christians. One mistake we can make is to think the basic pattern is that we gather to build each other up and then we scatter to do evangelism. But alongside our evangelistic efforts, we ought to be building up the existing members of the church when scattered.

It's striking how the New Testament instructions to the church often bleed into instructions for husbands and wives, parents and children, and masters and slaves. For example, 1 Peter 2 begins with general instructions about what it means to live as the people of God—as priests of God and the dwelling place of God. But then Peter continues with instructions about how slaves are to submit to their masters and how husbands and wives are to relate to each other. The implication is that being the people of God is lived out in the context of marriage and work relationships.

Similarly, in the first half of Ephesians Paul gives his theology of the church: they are the people chosen by God, reconciled by Christ and built together in Christ through the Holy Spirit. He then proceeds to talk about how members of the church are to relate to each other. Yet while he begins with general instructions for their life together as believers, by chapter 5 his focus has shifted to how they are to conduct themselves in other relationships, such as between husbands and wives, children and parents, and masters and slaves.

The same approach is found in Colossians 3, where Paul begins by speaking about the life of the body together:

> Let the peace of Christ rule in your hearts, since as members of one body you were called to peace. And be thankful. Let the message of Christ dwell among you richly as you teach

and admonish one another with all wisdom through psalms, hymns, and songs from the Spirit, singing to God with gratitude in your hearts. And whatever you do, whether in word or deed, do it all in the name of the Lord Jesus, giving thanks to God the Father through him. (Col 3:15-17)

From there, Paul moves directly to specific instructions for wives, husbands, children, fathers, slaves and masters (3:18-4:1).

Why is this? Surely it's because that's where people spend so much of their time. The majority of the Bible's instructions that relate to how we are to live as God's people or God's church are not about what we do when we're gathered, but about how to live in our daily relationships. That makes sense when you think about it: God is saying that how you live in those relationships affects the church. If you live out the gospel in those relationships, that will help build the church. If you fail to live out the gospel in those relationships, that will damage the church.

If you're married, one of the people you spend the most time with is your husband or wife. That represents one of your greatest ministry opportunities. The way that you live when you're with your spouse can either build them up in Christ for the blessing of God's church, or it can tear them down, discourage them, and make them ineffective in their Christian life.

The same is true for parents and children. While your children are young, you are the most important person in their lives in terms of discipling them in the Christian faith. If you're not doing it, it won't happen; you can't expect Sunday School teachers or youth leaders to do the heavy lifting of discipling your children when they only have 30-60 minutes a week with them while you have every day for 20 years or more. Moreover, it's important to recognize that you teach and train them not simply by what you say, but by how you live. If you tell them that we should live sacrificially and give generously, but then spend all your money on yourself, what lesson will they learn? If you say gathering every Sunday is crucial for the life of the church, but then you never turn up, what lesson will they learn?

But it's not only in family relationships that we have the opportunity to train and disciple brothers and sisters in Christ. Every relationship with another Christian, in whatever context, presents an opportunity for you to minister to them, to serve them and to build them up in the faith. Every relationship is an opportunity to reshape the way people think about God, life and the world by bringing biblical insight and wisdom to bear on your topics of conversation, whether that's politics, sport, money, possessions, or the way you use your time. Again, it's not simply about what you say, but about how you live. The way you live and act when you're around others will help to shape and train them, either in godliness or in ungodliness.

Of course, spending time with others is not only an opportunity for you to disciple them; it's also an opportunity for them to disciple you. I often encourage young couples to look around for parents in the church who do a good job raising their children and then to try and spend time with those parents to learn how to raise children for themselves. I encourage them to observe what they do (and don't do), and to ask them questions, so that they can be discipled in being godly parents themselves.

What is striking, however, is how little time churches spend in training and discipling people for the 'scattered' part of their life. Most ministry training in churches focuses exclusively on the three percent of the time that we're together, and overlooks the 97 percent of the time that we're off doing our own thing in the places where God in his wisdom has put us. We train Sunday

School teachers, but not parents. We train people to read the Bible in church, but not to read the Bible with their kids or friends. But that is profoundly short-sighted. Of course, we should equip people for the ways in which they serve the gathered church, but even more important is equipping people for their everyday lives. Pastors and church leaders need to make sure they focus on the 97 percent. But as church members we can all encourage our churches to have a proper balance. In doing that, we'll train an army of people to fulfil the task of the church in all sorts of different ways and all sorts of different places. We'll train them to love God, love the church, love their neighbours, and make disciples with their whole lives.

Sending workers

There is, however, one other important aspect of the church scattering: appointing and sending evangelists and gospel workers. As you read through the New Testament, you can't avoid the fact that the church not only calls on all its people to scatter and to follow and promote Christ wherever God has put them; it also appoints and sends specially chosen people.

We saw in the last chapter that the church in Acts 13, prompted by the Holy Spirit, sends out Paul (also called Saul) and Barnabas: "While they were worshiping the Lord and fasting, the Holy Spirit said, 'Set apart for me Barnabas and Saul for the work to which I have called them'" (Acts 13:2). Throughout Acts, many others are engaged in missionary work—people like Judas and Silas (15:22), Timothy (16:1-3), Priscilla and Aquila (18:18), Apollos (18:27) and Luke, the writer of Acts (20:13ff). Together, they give a picture of a growing band of gospel workers.

Similarly, throughout his letters Paul encourages the churches to support him and others in their gospel work. For example, he writes to the Romans, "I plan to [visit you] when I go to Spain. I hope to see you while passing through and to have you assist me on my journey there, after I have enjoyed your company for a while." (Rom 15:24) Jesus himself commands us to pray to this end. He says, "The harvest is plentiful, but the workers are few. Ask the Lord of the harvest, therefore, to send out workers into his harvest field." (Luke 10:2) We need to be praying that God would raise up workers for the harvest—workers who can be set apart by the church and sent out.

It's not enough simply to share the gospel ourselves. We need to be doing that, of course. But we also need to be raising up and sending people into gospel ministry. It's not one or the other, but both.

The relationship between gathering and scattering

But how does the scattering of the church relate to the gathering of the church? For one thing, why not always be scattered? Why don't we put all our efforts into that and forget about gathering together?

To answer those questions, we need to remember what we have already seen about the purpose of gathering. We gather together so that we might be built together into God's holy temple. The reason for gathering together is to equip God's people for works of service, to train and be trained in love and in the gospel, to be renewed by hearing God's word, to be encouraged amid the discouragements of our scattered ministry, to be brought to maturity in the faith, and to be brought to repentance for the sins that mar our lives and our ministries. We gather to be refocused on the grace and glory of God, to declare the praises of him who called us out of darkness, to be retrained to honour God, and to pray for each other in our ministries and in our pursuit of Christ in our work in the world. The point of gathering is so that when we scatter into the world, we go having been thoroughly equipped for the tasks that God has given us.

What does the church do? The church loves God, loves the church, loves its neighbours, and makes disciples. It does this by gathering to be built up in a holy faith, to be strengthened, to praise God and to pray. But it also does this by scattering and taking the love of Christ and the message of the gospel into the world and into the places where God in his wisdom has placed us.

6
GOD'S GIFTS
TO THE CHURCH

There's nothing worse than being assigned a task and then being left to flail around without the proper training or the proper resources. A friend of mine recently helped me build a raised veggie bed. He's a builder and I'm not. Left to myself, I could probably have worked out what needed to be done, but it would have taken me forever, and the result wouldn't have been great. What's more, I didn't have all the tools I needed, so I would have had to buy some or find places to borrow them. And I would have had to get the timber home in my small car. But when my friend came over, I didn't have to worry about any of that. He brought the timber on his trailer. He brought his tools to supplement my very limited collection. Most importantly, he brought his knowledge and expertise.

Yet I couldn't just sit back in my deckchair and watch him build the veggie bed for me. He put me to work carrying timber. He had me digging out the spot where the bed was to go. He gave me the impact driver and a big tub of screws and put me to work screwing the timber in place. In a couple of hours, we had a raised veggie bed. He brought the supplies, the tools and the expertise, but he got me working, showed me what to do, and trained me to do what I needed to do.

The church is very much the same. God not only gives us a task; he also gives us the supplies, the tools, the knowledge and the expertise that we need to do the job. The church is much less a DIY project with nothing more than a few YouTube videos for guidance; it's much more a weekend carpentry apprenticeship like the one I shared with my friend. Not only does God call the church into existence and give us a mission, but he gives us everything we need to do the task.

Jesus gives gifts to the church

One of the most important New Testament teachings for us to understand as we seek to carry out the church's mission is that God has given us gifts through his Spirit to do the good works he has prepared in advance for us to do. This idea is found in many places in the New Testament. For example, Paul tells the Ephesians:

> But to each one of us grace has been given as Christ apportioned it. This is why it says:
>
> "When he ascended on high,
> he took many captives
> and gave gifts to his people". (Eph 4:7-8)

So too, he writes to the Corinthians:

> Now to each one the manifestation of the Spirit is given for the common good. To one there is given through the Spirit

a message of wisdom, to another a message of knowledge by means of the same Spirit, to another faith by the same Spirit, to another gifts of healing by that one Spirit, to another miraculous powers, to another prophecy, to another distinguishing between spirits, to another speaking in different kinds of tongues, and to still another the interpretation of tongues. All these are the work of one and the same Spirit, and he distributes them to each one, just as he determines. (1 Cor 12:7-11)

A little earlier in 1 Corinthians, Paul has said, "I wish that all of you were as I am. But each of you has your own gift from God; one has this gift, another has that" (1 Cor 7:7).

Notice the expansiveness and all-inclusiveness of God's distribution of gifts: God gives gifts to "*each one* of us"; "to *each one* the manifestation of the Spirit is given"; he gives "to *each one*, just as he determines", which means that "*each of you* has your own gift from God". If you are a believer, then God has given you gifts. You might not feel particularly gifted, but you have gifts from God with which to serve him and serve his church. You have gifts with which to serve God and other people in the three percent of your time in the church, and you have gifts with which to serve God and other people in the 97 percent of time when you're scattered. You have gifts with which to encourage other believers, gifts to serve other believers in practical ways, gifts of money and time to give, gifts of leadership, gifts to raise your children, gifts to lead people in song, or gifts to disciple younger Christians.

As is so often the case, this truth is not hard to understand. The trick is to believe it. We can easily think that God has left us unequipped for the tasks he's given us. This belief often leads people to give up on ministries. But I'm not sure I've ever met anyone who's said, "I am thoroughly equipped for this ministry, and it perfectly suits me and my preferences". Parenting is a great example. Every parent I've ever met feels they are inadequate for the task, but that doesn't mean they should give up.

But look at what Paul could write to the Corinthians:

> I always thank my God for you because of his grace given you in Christ Jesus. For in him you have been enriched in every way—with all kinds of speech and with all knowledge—God thus confirming our testimony about Christ among you. Therefore you do not lack any spiritual gift as you eagerly wait for our Lord Jesus Christ to be revealed. (1 Cor 1:4-7)

The Corinthians were suffering from 'gift envy' (e.g. 1 Corinthians 12). There were people in the church with spectacular gifts, which left those without spectacular gifts feeling inferior and ill-equipped. But Paul tells them, "you do not lack any spiritual gift".

Paul is not talking primarily about staffing the church ministry teams. He's not saying that you'll always have enough Sunday School teachers and youth leaders. He's talking primarily about the gifts required to live the everyday Christian life. He's saying that God has given you the gifts to do the tasks he's called you to do. God has put you where you are, and he has given you what you need.

That doesn't mean that you have every gift that is available or that there's no room for growth. It does mean, however, that the gifts you have at the moment are precisely the gifts God wants you to have, and precisely the gifts that you need to do the good works that God has prepared for you to do. Moreover, he doesn't mean that you *personally* will have all the gifts within yourself. Paul is writing to a church. That whole church has all the gifts it needs. You almost certainly will not have every skill within yourself to be a wonderful parent, but within the church you will find that every gift you need is available and has been wonderfully provided by God. The "body of Christ" working together has everything that it needs "for the common good".

God gives all different kinds of gifts

This leads us to the next important idea: God has given us all different kinds of gifts. For example, as we saw above in Ephesians 4, not only has God given gifts through Jesus, but those gifts have been given *"as Christ apportioned"* (Eph 4:7). Similarly, in 1 Corinthians 12, we saw that God gives the same Holy Spirit to everyone who trusts in Jesus, but the manifestations of the Spirit's gifts work out differently in different people according to God's plan.

The same idea is present in Paul's letter to the Romans:

> For just as each of us has one body with many members, and these members do not all have the same function, so in Christ we, though many, form one body, and each member belongs to all the others. We have different gifts, according to the grace given to each of us. If your gift is prophesying, then prophesy in accordance with your faith; if it is serving, then serve; if it is teaching, then teach; if it is to encourage, then give encouragement; if it is giving, then give generously; if it is to lead, do it diligently; if it is to show mercy, do it cheerfully. (Rom 12:4-8)

Peter writes the same way in his first letter:

> Each of you should use whatever gift you have received to serve others, as faithful stewards of God's grace in its vari-

ous forms. If anyone speaks, they should do so as one who speaks the very words of God. If anyone serves, they should do so with the strength God provides ... (1 Pet 4:10-11)

So there are all different kinds of gifts. There are gifts of prophesying and tongues.[60] And there are gifts of serving, teaching, encouraging, contributing to the needs of others, leadership, and showing mercy, to name just a few.

Importantly, however, God's gifts are not simply skills; they are also opportunities and life circumstances. Or, perhaps more precisely, they are Spirit-given capacities that enable certain opportunities or life circumstances.

For example, Paul talks about his singleness as God's gift to him (1 Cor 7:7), a gift that includes not only the capacity to exercise self-control (7:9), but also the opportunities that singleness affords him. God's gift to him is not simply the gift of surviving singleness, but the opportunity to serve God in unique ways, not least by giving more time and attention to gospel ministry

---

60 The exact nature of the gifts of prophecy and tongues is a matter of significant debate. I take prophecy to be speaking words about Christ. As Revelation 19:10 notes, "it is the Spirit of prophecy who bears testimony to Jesus". That is, the key function of the Spirit, and of prophecy, is to make Christ and his gospel known—the gospel which was a mystery but has now been revealed in the Scriptures. Thus, while prophecy in the Old Testament was largely about what was to come in the person and work of Christ, now that Christ has come prophecy looks back more than forward. Thus in our context, prophecy is essentially speaking the truth of the gospel as we find it in the Bible. For a helpful discussion on prophecy, see chapter 3 in C Smith, *God's Good Design: What the Bible really says about men and women*, 2nd edn, Matthias Media, 2019, pp 55-82. I take speaking in tongues to be a miraculous gift of the Spirit that enables people to speak in a human language otherwise unknown to them for the purpose of making the gospel known. That was the miracle at Pentecost, when the apostles spoke languages they did not formerly know in order that their hearers might come to know Christ (Acts 2:1-12). In this way, both prophecy and tongues are gifts of the Spirit whose purpose is to make the gospel of Jesus Christ known among the nations.

(7:32-35).[61] By implication, then, marriage is God's gift to others. The gifts of singleness and marriage are opportunities to serve God and the church in different ways. The long and the short of it is, though, that God gives all kinds of different gifts to all kinds of different people as it pleases him.

Each of us will find ourselves fulfilling the Great Commandments and the Great Commission in different ways. We should all be loving God with all our heart, soul, mind and strength. We should all be loving our neighbours as ourselves. We should all be making disciples and teaching them to obey Jesus. But what that looks like for each of us will likely be quite different. The temptation that the Corinthian church faced and the temptation that we also face is to elevate some gifts above others, and hence to imply that we must all fulfil the Great Commandments and the Great Commission in exactly the same way. But Paul says that every gift that God gives is important for God's church to function properly. Yes, he tells the Corinthians to "eagerly desire the greater gifts" (12:31) and says they should "try to excel in those [gifts] that build up the church" (14:12). But that doesn't mean any Christian should feel bad or envious of the gifts of others. No gift that the Spirit gives for the building of God's church should be despised.

One of the most wonderful aspects of the church is its amazing diversity. It is beautiful that various people can pour a concrete slab, put up a roof, bake, cook, play music, teach, build a website, organize a bushwalk, run a board-game night, or start a conversation with a complete stranger. It's tempting to think that some of these are small or unimportant, but they're not. They are amazing

---

61 See JA Fitzmyer, *First Corinthians: A new translation with introduction and commentary*, AYBC, vol 32, Yale University Press, 2008, p 283.

gifts of God to the church. And God has apportioned gifts like these to each of us so that we can use them "for the common good"—to love God with every part of our being, to love our neighbours, to make disciples of all nations, and to teach them to obey all that Jesus has commanded.

God gives church leaders to equip the church

As well as giving gifts to each one of us, though, God has also given gifts to the church in the way of people who can equip us to use our gifts for the building up of the church. We've already seen above that Paul tells the Ephesian church that God has given gifts to the church. But what's interesting is that instead of going on to talk about the broader body, he focuses first on a few roles of church leadership: "So Christ himself gave the apostles, the prophets, the evangelists, the pastors and teachers, to equip his people for works of service ..." (Eph 4:11-12). God has not only given all kinds of different gifts to the church at large, but he's also given to the church people who are appointed to particular roles and offices so that they can equip the church members to use *their* gifts.

He mentions first the apostles and the prophets. Paul has said earlier (2:20) that these are the foundation on which the church is built. The idea seems to be that the church is built on the message of the apostles and either the message of the Old Testament prophets or the people who are sometimes called New Testament prophets—that is, the writers of the New Testament (like Jesus' brother James, Luke and Mark) who were not themselves apostles (as were men like Matthew and John).

Second are the pastors, teachers and evangelists. If the role of the apostles and prophets was to lay the foundation of the church, then the role of the evangelists, pastors and teachers is to continue building on that firm foundation in different but overlapping ways.

The evangelists continue the ministry of the apostles by focusing on taking the gospel to those who are not yet Christians. But their aim is not to do all that work themselves, but also to equip the rest of us to do the work. Without evangelists leading us in evangelism and training us for evangelism, the church easily becomes focused on itself. It becomes a domestic hospital whose aim it is to fluff up the pillows and make us feel better about ourselves, rather than being a war hospital whose aim is to patch us up and get us back out onto the front line of gospel proclamation.

Pastors or elders (the terms are largely interchangeable; see 1 Pet 5:1-5) continue the ministry of the apostles and prophets by shepherding people. We tend to have a very therapeutic vision of this role, seeing pastors as doing 'pastoral care'. The problem is that when most people hear the words 'pastoral care', they think of someone coming alongside them when they're sick or distressed to comfort them and listen to their problems. Certainly, caring for one another as Christians is a task in which we are all engaged. But the term 'pastor' comes from the Latin term for 'shepherd'. And the role of a shepherd is to lead people where Christ is going. It's about leading people in the truth, making sure they've grasped the gospel, protecting them from error, and calling them back from sin when they're wandering away from Jesus. Sometimes it can involve leading people in a direction they don't want to go. But it can also mean leading people who are going the right way and helping them to stay on track and keep growing.

The role of teachers, however, is more specifically to build on the foundation of the apostles and prophets by continuing to teach God's people the truth so that they can build each other up in the truth. Teachers seem to be those who are set aside by the church for the specific task of grounding people in the truth. The great theologian of the Reformation, John Calvin, called them the "doctors" of the church—not in the sense of medical doctors, but of lecturers or professors who equip the people with the truth for their daily lives of living for Jesus.

Sometimes, pastors and teachers are taken together as the same thing. And the two functions certainly overlap. But there's reason to believe that there is some important difference between them. Like the difference between pastors and evangelists, the difference lies not so much in the tools of their trade—things like the gospel, prayer and love. Nor does it lie in the breadth of their ministry—an evangelist should be able to lead, a pastor should be able to teach, and a teacher should be able to evangelize. Rather, the difference seems to lie in their focus: pastors focus on leading, caring for and overseeing the flock; teachers focus on teaching the truth and correcting error; and evangelists focus on making new disciples.

That said, it is important to remember that the role of these Christian leaders is not simply to do all the work, but to equip *us*—to equip all God's people—to perform "works of service" and to use the gifts that God has given us. The apostles and prophets train us 'from a distance' through the words that God spoke through them and caused to be written down for us in the Bible. Studying the words of the Bible equips us for every good work, for every ministry and every work of service for Christ that we will ever do (2 Tim 3:17). The evangelists, pastors and teachers equip us more directly: they teach us the word; they shepherd us by the word and call us back to repentance and faith; they model to us a godly life and ministry; they equip us for evangelism in our homes, in our community groups, and in our workplaces. Their task is not to do all the work for us, but to train us.

Let's look again at a diagram of gospel ministry found in *The Vine Project*:[62]

Rescued and transformed

Domain of darkness
engage » evangelize »

Kingdom of the Son
» establish » equip

By their preaching, training and example,
pastors equip every Christian to help those
around them take a step to the right

A redeemed
people gathered
around the risen
Christ

The diagram shows that the task of the church is to make mature disciples by engaging and evangelizing those who don't know God, and by establishing and equipping those who have received Jesus by faith. But, as the diagram highlights, that task is not simply for the pastors. Rather, in line with Ephesians 4, the role of the pastors is to equip every Christian to be involved in the work of engaging, evangelizing, establishing and equipping.

Imagine if a tradesman took on a new apprentice, but the apprentice turned up to work, sat down, and watched their trainer do all their work: cutting timber, running cables and concreting. It would be outrageous. The whole point of an apprenticeship is to be trained and equipped to work, to serve, and to learn the business. In the same way, pastors, teachers and evangelists are God's gifts to the church, not so we can sit on deckchairs, but so we can be trained and equipped to serve God better, both in the church and in the places where he scatters us in our daily lives.

---

62 Marshall and Payne, *The Vine Project*, p 148. Diagram reproduced with permission.

God's gifts are for building the church

But why has God given us these gifts through his Spirit? This is where Paul turns next in Ephesians 4. God has given the apostles, prophets, pastors, teachers and evangelists ...

> ... to equip his people for works of service, so that the body of Christ may be built up until we all reach unity in the faith and in the knowledge of the Son of God and become mature, attaining to the whole measure of the fullness of Christ.
>
> Then we will no longer be infants, tossed back and forth by the waves, and blown here and there by every wind of teaching and by the cunning and craftiness of people in their deceitful scheming. Instead, speaking the truth in love, we will grow to become in every respect the mature body of him who is the head, that is, Christ. From him the whole body, joined and held together by every supporting liga-ment, grows and builds itself up in love, as each part does its work. (Eph 4:12-16)

The reason God gives these gifts to the church is so that the church might be built up into maturity. It's so that we won't be led astray by every crazy doctrine that comes around. It's so that we'll speak the truth in love and grow up into the likeness of Christ. And it's so that we'll grow in love for each other as we each do our part.

Whenever we think about gifts, it's easy to forget that their purpose is not so that *I*, the gifted one, can be built up, but so that *the church* can be built up. It's not first and foremost about me finding my ministry area, but about the church and the growth of Jesus' body. Remember, Paul says that the gifts we receive are "for the common good" (1 Cor 12:7). He says that, because we belong to a body, our gifts and even our very selves belong to each other

(Rom 12:3-8). That's quite challenging for Western individualists who think we belong to ourselves.

Singleness is a great example. Some people choose singleness for the sake of serving the kingdom. But some people have singleness 'thrust upon them', as it were; they would love to be married, and they find being single very difficult. It's a 'gift' they would never have chosen for themselves. But your singleness, whether or not you chose it, is God's gift *to the church*. God has given you this gift so that you can love the church and build the church. Viewed through the prism of how the gift benefits the individual, it becomes very hard to understand the positives of being 'left on the shelf'. After all, being single can make life much harder in many ways. But viewed through the prism of how the gift benefits the body of Christ, it becomes clear how something like singleness might be a good gift. This perspective helps us to see how singleness is also a good gift to the individual, since using that gift in the service of God and others is one of the ways that we find joy. That doesn't mean it's wrong for a single man or woman to want to get married or to seek to get married. But it does change the way we view our gifts and our life situations.

Or take another example: you might absolutely hate administrative or organizational work, yet you also happen to be ridiculously good at it. God has given you those gifts so that you can love the church, serve the church, and build the church. What a blessing to you and to the church! If you happen to enjoy it as well, that's a double blessing.

Another mistake we often make when thinking about God's gifts to us is to see them a bit like presents from God that we can stuff under the bed and pull out when we feel like using them. We tend to use our gifts and serve others in ways that satisfy us or ways that we find rewarding. Or we use our gifts in ways and at times that are convenient for us. But that's not why God has given us gifts. The gifts God has given us are for serving him and for serving his people in the place and in the church where God has put us. To fail to use those gifts and to keep them for ourselves fails to recognize why God has given them to us.

That's what Jesus' parable of the "bags of gold" (Matt 25:14-30) is about. Jesus tells the story of a man who entrusts his servants with extraordinary amounts of money. Two of the servants use the money that has been entrusted to them, making a healthy profit. And their master further rewards them for their diligent use of what he entrusted to them. But one of the servants buries his money in the ground. When the master returns, he takes away from that servant even the relatively little that he had. Through this parable, Jesus teaches us that we'll be held to account on the last day for how we've used what God has entrusted to us. Of course, God has entrusted to us all manner of gifts in the form of abilities, time and opportunities, as well as the very message of the gospel itself.[63]

The great purpose of the church is to build—to build itself using the gifts God has given us. And that is a task in which we are all involved. It's not really possible to be part of the church and to not be involved in building. The way you build might not be very noticeable; it might be very modest. But in the normal course of events, every Christian will be part of a local church and will be building.

But, once again, we must be careful not to make the three percent more important than the 97 percent. Jesus has apportioned gifts to us through his Spirit not simply so that we can exercise them for the small fraction of our lives when we're gathered

63 RT France, *The Gospel of Matthew*, NICNT, Eerdmans, 2007, pp 951-952.

together. He has also given them to us for building in the other 97 percent of our lives. Bigger than the question of how you're building the church on Sunday, or in your small group, is the question of how you're building in the rest of your life.

Church and consumerism

Nevertheless, although the time we spend gathered together as a church only accounts for a small portion of our time, the idea that God has given each of us gifts for building the church is crucial to grasp, since it reframes how we think about the time we spend gathered together. Most importantly, it overturns the consumerist view of the church that seems so prevalent in many churches.

The term 'consumerism' is typically connected with possessions—buying more and more stuff and satisfying every desire we have. That kind of consumerism is an enormous issue in our society, and Christians can certainly be sucked into that. But there's another kind of consumerism that can affect the church. More generally, consumerism is about taking, and taking simply to satisfy yourself. It is about receiving rather than giving. And that attitude often affects the church—people become consumers of church rather than members, partners and co-workers.

That kind of consumerism manifests itself in many ways in the life of the church. It manifests itself in 'church shopping', where consumerism asks the question, "Which church suits me best?" rather than "Where has God placed me to serve?" Consumerism manifests in people opting in and out as it suits them: "Church doesn't suit me today, so I won't go" or "Church doesn't suit the kids today, so I won't go" or "Church in that form doesn't suit me" or "That small group doesn't suit me because the people are not like me" or "Prayer meetings are too tiring, so I won't go" or

"Fellowship meals are too awkward, so I won't stay". Consumerism manifests itself in people coming to church to engage with God but not with anyone else. Consumerism sits at church in an imaginary cubicle and avoids any contact with any other people. Consumerism turns up late and runs out the door when church finishes. In the consumerist view of the church, individuals simply turn up and absorb what they need, then they each go their separate ways.

But the problem with consumerism is that it's completely at odds with the gospel. Yes, the gospel is a gospel of grace. We come empty-handed to receive everything as a gracious gift from God. We come to drink deeply from the well of God's grace. We come to buy without money (Isa 55:1) and to eat the bread of life which is Jesus himself (John 6:48-51). The gospel is a gospel of generous consumption. But it is a gospel in which we receive *in order that we might give*. Jesus says, "Freely you have received; freely give" (Matt 10:8). Consumerism is at odds with the gospel, and it is at odds with the church.

When COVID first forced churches to close and move online, my church made a conscious decision to only video the sermon, not the entire gathering. Part of the reason was to push back against the idea that you could just sit down on your lounge, switch on the TV and consume—watch the songs, the prayers and the sermon—and then just get up and get on with the rest of your life. In our model, church members could sit and listen to the sermon, but the other parts of a regular Sunday gathering—the songs, the prayers, the Sunday School lessons—required people to take some initiative for their engagement and their spiritual growth, and for the growth of those in their households.

But as we did that, it raised a very important question: why would we push back against simply consuming church online, but not against simply consuming church in person? What if we structured church so that you couldn't simply turn up, but you had to engage in building others up? What if we asked something of people—maybe not much, but something, even something small? What if asking every person to contribute to building the church in a small way was at the heart of how we structured our gatherings? After all, that's at the heart of the New Testament's picture of church, so how can we not do that when we're together?

Once we were able to gather in person again, we decided to do this by breaking up into small groups in the middle and at the end of our gathering to pray together and to reflect on the sermon together. It's not much, and there may have been other ways to achieve the same objective. But it was a small attempt to push back on the idea that you can rock up to church, sit down, consume, and then run out the door at the end. It was a small attempt to encourage people to start coming to church and building with whatever gifts God has given them, to whatever degree they are able. Because at the heart of Christianity and faith in Jesus is not just consuming, but building.

The shape of gospel ministry

It needs to be said, however, that even when we are using the gifts that God has entrusted to us, it will not always be easy. That's important to say because we often confuse giftedness with effortlessness. Part of the reason we often feel we don't have the gifts to do something is because we think that if we were gifted, we would find it easy. If we find it to be hard work, then we think we mustn't have the gifts. But to be gifted by the Holy Spirit to serve Jesus does not mean the task will be effortless. In fact, the Bible teaches us that it will often be hard work.

Paul speaks about this reality in 2 Corinthians, where he begins a description of his ministry with these words: "Therefore, since through God's mercy we have this ministry, we do not lose heart" (2 Cor 4:1; cf. v 16). The implication, of course, is that losing heart in gospel ministry is easily done. And reading through Paul's description of his ministry reveals why that might be:

> But we have this treasure in jars of clay to show that this all-surpassing power is from God and not from us. We are hard pressed on every side, but not crushed; perplexed, but not in despair; persecuted, but not abandoned; struck down, but not destroyed. (4:7-9)

The "treasure" Paul is referring to is the good news of what God has done in Jesus. The "jar of clay" is his own body. Paul says that his gospel ministry has been hard and perplexing; it has resulted in persecution; it has seen him "struck down". Later he says:

> As servants of God we commend ourselves in every way: in great endurance; in troubles, hardships and distresses; in beatings, imprisonments and riots; in hard work, sleepless nights and hunger; in purity, understanding, patience and kindness; in the Holy Spirit and in sincere love; in truthful speech and in the power of God; with weapons of righteousness in the right hand and in the left; through glory and dishonour, bad report and good report; genuine, yet regarded as impostors; known, yet regarded as unknown; dying, and yet we live on; beaten, and yet not killed; sorrowful, yet always rejoicing; poor, yet making many rich; having nothing, and yet possessing everything. (6:4-10)

Near the end of the letter, he offers another list of hardships that involves things like prison, beatings, shipwreck, long hours and hunger, to name just a few (11:23-28). But not even those difficulties capture the most significant cost of his ministry:

> We always carry around in our body the death of Jesus, so that the life of Jesus may also be revealed in our body. For we who are alive are always being given over to death for Jesus' sake, so that his life may also be revealed in our mortal body. So then, death is at work in us, but life is at work in you. (4:10-12)

Paul's ministry is cross-shaped. He always carries around the death of Jesus. And this costly ministry is no accident; it's not that Paul is a bit of a ministry failure. His ministry is costly because that was the shape of Jesus' ministry, and Jesus has called each of his people to follow him on that path in their own life and ministry. As we point to the crucified Saviour, our lives refract just a small sample of Jesus' own suffering in our place. Paul says that the reason for this hardship is "to show that this all-surpassing power is from God and not from us" (4:7). If using the gifts God has given us in the service of his kingdom was not cross-shaped, then people might think the power belonged to us. But God's purpose is that the gospel be communicated through "jars of clay" so that people will know that it is God's power that saves, not our power.

No ministry you ever do will be without some form of suffering. It may come in the form of opposition or criticism, in the form of persecution, or in the form of perplexity and confusion over why your best-laid plans and efforts don't seem to work. Yet whatever form your suffering takes, these challenges and difficulties will always be present, because that is God's plan.

Nevertheless, gospel ministry is not simply cross-shaped; it is *cross-and-resurrection-shaped*. Paul says he is given over to death so that the life of Jesus might be revealed: "death is at work *in us*, but life is at work *in you*" (4:12).

Even though using the gifts God has given us will be difficult and challenging at times, there is glory and wonder here: through this ministry, people find life in Jesus. Through God's people speaking simple words about Jesus, "the light of the knowledge of God's glory [is] displayed in the face of Christ" (4:6). Paul says that when we speak words about Jesus, it is like God speaking the world into existence—empowered by the Spirit, our simple and ordinary gospel words can make light shine in the darkness of people's hearts so that they see the truth of the gospel.

When you speak to your neighbour about Jesus and find it plain, awkward and powerless, the truth is that through simple situations like this, God calls people to faith in Jesus. When you teach Sunday School and half the kids are mucking up while the other half are staring out the window, and you come home wondering whether all your work is achieving anything, remember that in such weakness God's power is made perfect. When you go out on a limb and invite a friend to read the Bible with you, even when you've never done anything like that before and you feel hopelessly ill-equipped, trust that the same God who spoke the world into existence only with words can use your simple efforts to shine his light into your friend's heart.

Using the gifts that God has entrusted to us to serve him and his kingdom will be difficult, awkward and strange. Invariably, it will cost us. Frequently, it will cause us to suffer. But through it, others will find life in Jesus. Death will be at work in us, but life will be at work in them.

7
THE CHURCH AND REST

It might seem peculiar to have a chapter on rest in a book on the church, but over time I've become more and more convinced that our failure to understand rest is having an enormous impact on the way we live and work as God's church. Even before COVID, it was relatively clear that many people were facing a crisis of rest. People seemed overwhelmingly busy and often looked exhausted. COVID seems only to have confirmed that.

One of the reflections lots of people have made about COVID has been the opportunity they've found just to rest, to not be so busy and to not be racing out of the house, running from one thing to another. The lack of rest has become such an issue that even secular writers are starting to talk about a secular Sabbath.[64]

---

64 See, for example, P Iyer, 'Why we need to slow down our lives', *ideas.ted.com*, 4 November 2014, accessed 1 February 2022 (ideas.ted.com/why-we-need-a-secular-sabbath); and E Meyer, 'The way we're working isn't working. What can we do about it?', *Ambition & Balance*, 13 August 2019, accessed 1 February 2022 (blog.doist.com/way-we-work-isnt-working).

I am increasingly convinced that without addressing the crisis of rest, it will be hard to move forward.

But rest is not simply an individual exercise. Rest, properly understood from the Bible's perspective, is a shared activity—it's a *church* activity. In this final chapter, I want to think with you a little bit about rest and show you its place as a vital part of the life of the church.

Before we think about rest and the church, let's think more generally about the Bible's teaching on this topic, starting back in the Old Testament.

The gift nobody wants

It might seem extraordinary, but in the Old Testament resting was a command. Why would anyone ever need to be *commanded* to rest? You would think that people would need to be commanded to work. And yet twice in the Old Testament, in the Ten Commandments—God's dot-point summary of what it means to live in relationship with him—God says resting is up there as one of the most important aspects.

On the first occasion, God has just brought the people out of Egypt to himself, when he says:

> Remember the Sabbath day by keeping it holy. Six days you shall labour and do all your work, but the seventh day is a sabbath to the LORD your God. On it you shall not do any work, neither you, nor your son or daughter, nor your male or female servant, nor your animals, nor any foreigner residing in your towns. For in six days the LORD made the heavens and the earth, the sea, and all that is in them, but he rested on the seventh day. Therefore the LORD blessed the Sabbath day and made it holy. (Exod 20:8-11)

On the second occasion, God is about to bring the people into the promised land, and Moses reminds the people of the Ten Commandments, including the command about the Sabbath (Deut 5:12-15). Both passages explain what is called the "Sabbath", which literally means 'rest'. According to God's command, the people were to rest completely from their labours one day in every seven.

In the Old Testament, that Sabbath command was central to the life of God's people—so much so that it's described as the sign of God's covenant with the people through Moses (Exod 31:12-17). The Sabbath exemplifies the nature of the relationship between God and the people: it is God who makes the people holy, not the people who make themselves holy (Exod 31:13). To reject the Sabbath was essentially to reject God himself and his gift of grace.

Moreover, the Sabbath was not simply one command; it was a principle that worked its way out in a variety of other commands about rest and celebration. So God not only gave the people the weekly Sabbath, but also gave them annual feast days when they were to rest (e.g. Leviticus 23). They even had a whole year off every seven years (Lev 25:1-7), while every 50 years they had two years off (Lev 25:8-55)! In other words, God is really, really big on rest—extravagantly so, you might even say. If God was running the government or a business today, some of us would probably accuse him of being too easygoing. After all, weren't we made to work (Gen 2:15)? Yet God loves rest in its proper place.

But what is the place of the Sabbath and rest in the New Testament era? Let's begin with Romans 14, where Paul says that we no longer need to hold any day as special above any other day. "One person considers one day more sacred than another; another considers every day alike. Each of them should be fully convinced in their own mind" (Rom 14:5). Not only that, but the book of Hebrews also tells us that the Sabbath was a sign of something greater: an eternal rest with God.

> There remains, then, a Sabbath-rest for the people of God; for anyone who enters God's rest also rests from their works, just as God did from his. Let us, therefore, make every effort to enter that rest, so that no-one will perish by following their example of disobedience. (Heb 4:9-11)

Hebrews also tells us that the old covenant, of which the Sabbath was a key sign, is obsolete and disappearing (Heb 8:13).

But while all that is true, it's also important to recognize that the pattern of one day's rest in seven is not primarily grounded in God's covenant with the people through Moses. Rather, it's a pattern established in creation. The Bible's story of rest begins long before either Exodus or Deuteronomy; it begins at the creation of the world. In Genesis 1, we read how God created the world in six days. But then we're told that on the seventh day he rested from all his labour (Gen 2:1-3) and set it apart as a special day: "Then God blessed the seventh day and made it holy, because on it he rested from all the work of creating that he had done" (Gen 2:3). In that sense, the Sabbath is not first and foremost a law. It's part of the very fabric of creation. When the Sabbath law is given in Exodus 20, then, it is not introducing something new, but rather codifying a principle that God had established in his creation of the world.

So although there's a greater, eternal rest to which the Sabbath pointed and which we are invited to enter, that doesn't mean we don't need weekly rest anymore. Some people today hold the view that although God was extravagantly generous in the Old Testament in giving people rest, the 'good news' of the New Testament is that now we get to work 24/7. Such a view, however, fails to properly understand where we are on the biblical timeline. It fails to understand that we remain 'enfleshed' in the first creation. One day of rest in seven was not simply an arbitrary rule that God made. On the contrary, it is part of the pattern and fabric of the world. It is how the world and the people living in it were made to function.

There is, therefore, still a physical, emotional and spiritual need to rest.

In fact, not only do we *need* to rest; Jesus tells us that rest is God's *gift* to us. Jesus tells a group of Pharisees that "the Sabbath was made for man, not man for the Sabbath" (Mark 2:27). That is, God made the Sabbath as a gift for us—for our benefit. The religious leaders of Jesus' day had turned the Sabbath into a straitjacket of rules to which people needed to conform. But that was not God's purpose in the Sabbath. The pattern of one whole day of rest every week is a gift from God to be received with gladness.

Nevertheless, given how few of us take the opportunity to really rest, you could think that the whole idea of rest is an enormous burden we'd be better off without.

Sometimes when I talk to people about our human need to rest and God's gracious gift of regular rest, a look of sheer panic and terror comes across their face—as though the thought of not doing whatever their heart is set on is an unimaginable nightmare. How strange this is when we all feel so busy and so overwhelmed. It would seem there is something deeply wrong with our hearts—something that makes resting very hard for us.[65] The Sabbath is

---

65 Similarly, many of the activities we do to 'rest' are not especially restful. I remember once spending my day off mountain-bike riding. By the time I'd driven to where we were going, ridden for half the day and driven home, I was thoroughly exhausted. That exhaustion lasted through the rest of the week. A good question to ask of rest is "Will this be restful?" If it won't be, find another time to do it.

God's gift to us, but it's a gift that very few of us know how to receive or even want to receive.

The heart of rest

But we still need to ask: What does it mean to rest? Often, we think of rest as simply not doing anything that counts as work. But biblical rest is far more than that. And unless we understand the heart of rest, we won't be able to really and truly rest.

When we look back at God's rest in Genesis 1, we find that at the heart of what God did was enjoyment of all his work. At the end of every day of creation, God looked back and celebrated what he'd done. We're told repeatedly that "God saw that it was good" (Gen 1:10, 12, 18, 21, 25). Then, at the end of the sixth day, creation was completed, and God rested:

> God saw all that he had made, and it was *very good*. And there was evening, and there was morning—the sixth day.
>
> Thus the heavens and the earth were completed in all their vast array.
>
> By the seventh day God had finished the work he had been doing; so on the seventh day he rested from all his work. Then God blessed the seventh day and made it holy, because on it he rested from all the work of creating that he had done. (Gen 1:31-2:3)

The seventh day acts as a kind of capstone on God's work of creation. God stops his work, looks back at all that he has made, considers it, and affirms its goodness. As one scholar notes, these actions convey "enjoyment, approval and delight" on God's part.[66] Or in the words of Psalm 104, a Psalm about God's work of creation: "May the Lord rejoice in all his works" (Ps 104:31). God's pattern in creation then becomes the pattern for our rest also. Look again at what God said as he gave the commandment about the Sabbath:

> Remember the Sabbath day by keeping it holy … For in six days the LORD made the heavens and the earth, the sea, and all that is in them, but he rested on the seventh day. Therefore the LORD blessed the Sabbath day and made it holy. (Exod 20:8, 11)

So the point is not simply for us to follow God's practice of one day of rest in seven. At the heart of our rest ought to be looking back and enjoying all God's work, not least his work in creation.

God has made a glorious world for us to enjoy to his glory. We ought not to feel guilty about enjoying it. In fact, God is honoured when we enjoy it. But rest doesn't simply mean enjoying the world and life, but enjoying it *as a means to the end of enjoying God*. The chief end and purpose of every human, as the Westminster Catechism highlights, is "to glorify God, and to enjoy him forever". That, too, is the great purpose of our rest. That might mean, for example, going for a walk with family and friends to enjoy nature—but not simply to enjoy nature, but to enjoy it with the purpose of enjoying God and giving thanks to God for the birds and the trees and the fresh air and the sun and the rain.

Our lives are often so compressed that we never stop to delight in God. Even our enjoyment is often a relentless pursuit where we squeeze in as much as we can to tick off items from a bucket list.

---

66 CJ Collins, *Genesis 1-4: A linguistic, literary, and theological commentary*, P&R, 2006, p 71.

But when we live that way, we don't rest because we don't enjoy God. We go away on holidays and come back more tired than before. We finally reach the weekend only to return to work more exhausted than we were on Friday. God's gift of a day of rest is an opportunity to stop and to direct our minds to relating with and enjoying God.

But our day of rest is also an opportunity to stop and look back at what God has done *through us* in the past week. Again, we are often so consumed by everything that still needs to be done and that we want to achieve that we can never stop to enjoy what God has already enabled us to do. Many people today tell me that they struggle to keep focused on the task at hand; their mind is often racing ahead to the ten things they still need to do. But in God's grace, he has given us one day where we can actively break that cycle of relentless activity, of relentless pursuit—a day when we can stop, not to think about what still needs to be done, but to celebrate what has been done.

So rest looks back and delights in what God has done in creation, and even to what he has done through us in this past week. But Deuteronomy 5 gives a different justification for the Sabbath. God says:

> Observe the Sabbath day by keeping it holy ... Remember that you were slaves in Egypt and that the LORD your God brought you out of there with a mighty hand and an outstretched arm. Therefore the LORD your God has commanded you to observe the Sabbath day. (Deut 5:12, 15)

In Deuteronomy, the people are called to look back and reflect. They had been slaves in Egypt, but God had redeemed them. Again, at the heart of the command to rest is reflection and delight in what God has done. But in Deuteronomy that reflection and delight is not simply in the work of creation, but in the work of redemption and recreation.

We need to pause from our work and from the pursuit of our lives to remember and delight in what God has done in redeeming us from sin. We need to remember and enjoy the fact that God sent Jesus to die in our place, to rise again for our justification, and to send his Spirit to dwell in us.

This is one of the aims in gathering together as a church. As we've seen in chapter 4, the church comes together to be reminded of God's great gospel work, to declare his praises, and to express its dependence on him in prayer. These are all aspects of rest. We come together to leave behind all our other preoccupations and to focus on God's grace and goodness. We come together to point each other again to the grace and glory of God in both creation and redemption. We come to have our hearts lifted up so that we can carry our renewed hope in the gospel with us into a new week. In God's great pattern of creation, we need that recalibration not just once a year, not just once a month, not just some weeks when we can manage the time; we need it every week.

We need it, too, not just for a couple of hours while we're together. We also need to set aside a whole day for it. God has given us a *day*, not simply a few hours in a day, to remember and delight in all that he has done.

For most of us, it makes sense for that day to be the same day that we gather with our brothers and sisters. But this is not essential. For example, Sunday will always be so busy for pastors that it makes sense to set aside another day for rest. Whatever day of the week we choose, the point is that we need to recapture the practice of setting aside a whole day for enjoying God. That doesn't mean that you have to spend every moment with your nose in the Bible. But it does mean that it's a day when your focus and energy are geared towards delight and joy in God.

If we think of rest merely as resting from activity, we'll miss the heart of rest and we won't gain the greatest benefit that God offers us. God's great gift is rest, both from our work and from our bucket lists, so that we might teach our hearts to delight in him. That is his most precious gift to us. That is what we most need—not simply to stop working, but to start worshipping.

Rest in church

But if rest is part of the weekly rhythm of life, and if rest so that we can delight in God is a key part of our time together, then we need to ask the very important question about whether our times together are really structured to be restful in that sense.

For some years now, I've been deeply concerned about the 'complexification' of church. For many, gathering for church has become so complicated, difficult and cumbersome that it's not really restful anymore. It's become a kind of industry.

We often do that to ourselves with our expectations. We can end up feeling that everything needs to be 'excellent'. And while it's true that we should joyfully seek to do things well in service of God and others, the potential downside is that Sunday gatherings can become massive performances that require huge amounts of organization and practice. A friend of mine told me that when she was rostered on sound at her church, she needed to be there two hours before the meeting started for rehearsal. Everything needed to be polished, and that required hours of practice.

But is that the only way? Is that the best way?

What if, instead of ministering out of hours of practice, we ministered out of a lifetime of being shaped by God's word and prayer? What if we accepted that at the heart of church are messy and weak people who've been called together by the gospel and filled with the Spirit, who gather together every week to build each other up with the gifts God has given them, but who will rarely do that perfectly? What if we considered weakness as an opportunity for God to display his power rather than an embarrassment that needed to be stamped out? What if we accepted that at the heart of the gathered church are the very ordinary practices of hearing the word read, explained and applied to our hearts, praying with one another, reflecting together, exhorting and encouraging one another, and singing together (even if the songs are really old, really simple and completely unaccompanied, and we're not very good singers)? What if we accepted that those simple practices are absolutely life-changing because they're God's means of grace by which he's promised to build and strengthen his church and build us together in love and good deeds?

I'm not suggesting that we should never seek to grow and improve in what we do. We should. But resting in God means learning to accept that where we are today is more than enough for God to work through. If we adopted that kind of attitude to our church gatherings, it would make them less of a burden and more restful—not because we're 'slacking off', but because we're focusing on the kind of rest that really matters.

One of the questions I've been asking myself through COVID (largely because it has been a necessity) is how we can serve each other without lots of planning and preparation, but in ways that are still rich—possibly even richer than what we've been doing. There are many aspects of church life that we simply take for granted but which can take huge amounts of time and preparation from people who are already busy serving God through the week in many important ways.

What's interesting, though, is that during COVID we were

forced to get along without some of those things we'd come to see as indispensable. We've discovered that you can run music on a shoestring. You can even sing along to recorded music. You can do without coffee or morning tea after church. You can even do without crèche or Sunday School. Sure, it's taken some adjustment, and some of these enforced changes have caused real difficulties. But good things have come out of it. One person told me how their four-year-old daughter prayed during group prayers. Another shared how their son, who has learning difficulties, could contribute his insights from the sermon in the time of sermon reflection. Someone else noted that when Sunday School wasn't running, they were much more intentional about discipling their children at home.

Again, I'm not suggesting that 'the COVID way' is the right way or the best way, but it certainly invites us to ask important questions about what we do and whether we might be able to strive for the same goals in ways that require less busyness.

Church doesn't always need to be complicated. Sometimes we make it complicated. What matters is gathering together under God's word to listen to God, to pray together, to sing, and to be built up and refreshed by the gospel, so that we can go out into the places where God has put us to serve him.[67]

Rest and the cross

There is, however, something even more crucial to receiving rest. And this, perhaps more than anything else, is essential for living

---

67 Our performance and excellence culture also has implications for church plant-ing. If everything about church gatherings needs to be 'excellent', planting a new church is a high bar. If I just need the word and prayer, I can plant a church almost at the drop of a hat.

as a community at rest. If we don't take this final step, it doesn't matter how restful we try to make church or our days off, because we'll still miss the boat.

One of the most famous and most comforting passages about rest in the Bible comes from Jesus himself, who says this to us:

"Come to me, all you who are weary and burdened, and I will give you rest. Take my yoke upon you and learn from me, for I am gentle and humble in heart, and you will find rest for your souls. For my yoke is easy and my burden is light." (Matt 11:28-30)

Jesus says that if we come to him, he will give us rest. Nevertheless, somewhat unexpectedly, receiving that rest means taking Jesus' yoke upon ourselves.

A yoke was used to make carrying a burden easier. It was used to tie two oxen together so they could pull a cart. A different kind of yoke could also be used to help a person carry, say, a couple of buckets of water or grain.[68] The point is that to receive the help on offer, you need to take something onto yourself. As Christians, that 'something' is Jesus and his yoke. In other words, the rest that Jesus offers us comes at a cost. It comes at the cost of giving up our lives to Christ as we take on his yoke.

I once heard someone say that the most tiring thing in our lives is sin. That's true. And the most tiring sin, which is really the heart of every sin, is hanging onto our lives and trying to keep them for ourselves. We think that giving up our lives to Jesus will be exhausting and keeping our lives for ourselves will be restful. But it's the exact opposite. Jesus said, "For whoever wants to save their life will lose it, but whoever loses their life for me and for

---

68 See France, *The Gospel of Matthew*, p 449.

the gospel will save it" (Mark 8:35).

When I talk with people, I often discover that their 'non-working' lives tend to be as crammed with activity as their working lives. In fact, these days it's probably their non-working lives that are *more crammed* with activity. So many of us try to squeeze as much as possible into every spare minute. Often that's in pursuit of personal goals: fitness, reading more books, enjoyment, getting better at soccer, winning the next competition, finishing the next project, remodelling the spare room, repainting the back deck or spending time with friends. But while these might all be things you would like to do, they're not necessarily all things that God wants you to do. In fact, God may not want you to do any of them.[69] Yet we find it almost impossible to give them up.

What exhausts us is our restless pursuit of ambition, achievement and self-interest. The chilling consequence of that, then, is that no matter how much we reconfigure our weekly gatherings, they will never be restful, because gathering with other Christians fundamentally conflicts with our ambitions. Church impedes our ambition, our achievement and our opportunity to satisfy ourselves. But the problem is not simply one of time—not enough time in the week to achieve our ambitions. The problem is also one of heart-space: unless we give up the love of ourselves and our desire to achieve all our dreams, there won't be any space left in our hearts for God. There will be no space for the rest that comes

---

69 Frequently, when I have conversations with people about rest, they inevitably say something like, "But I think we each need to work out what is genuinely restful for us". That's true to some degree. But I suspect that often we use this kind of argument as a justification for our restless pursuit of our ambitions: "I find renovating the house 'restful', therefore it's okay to exhaust myself renovating the house". Maybe so, but in our culture of achievement and the endless pursuit of entertainment, we need to learn to rest from our ambitions and our endless desire to satisfy ourselves.

from enjoying and delighting in God. Until we can give up our ambitions, achievement, self-interest, and even our very lives to God and take up Jesus' yoke, we will be unable to find true rest.[70]

Giving up those dreams, hopes and aspirations will be easier if we realize that we do not need to cram every experience and dream into this world. An eternity with God awaits us. We don't need to get everything done today or this weekend or this year. We can afford to rest and be still.

But not only should we give up our ambitions and our lives to Jesus daily (cf. Luke 9:23); there seems to be something profoundly important about taking a particular day every week to stop and consciously give up our lives to Jesus—to say to God, "Here, Lord, take my life. It's yours to do with as you will."

This, too, is a key part of what we do when we gather together as church. Even the simple act of turning up to gather with God's people and direct your attention to God is a subversive act that undermines your own personal hopes and dreams. At least, that is, with respect to the hours spent at church that you could have used to sleep in, go surfing, play sport or whatever else you enjoy doing. Meeting together to serve one another subverts our self-focused culture; it subverts our personal desires and ambitions. It reminds us that life is more than *me*. Paradoxically, then, serving others can be unexpectedly restful in a profound way.

But even more importantly, what we hear and do when we gather with our brothers and sisters under the word of God reshapes our minds and our aspirations. Recently at our church, a

---

70 There is a sense, then, in which we need to also rest *for* our church gatherings. If we gather together after a week crammed full of various things and with a checklist of more to do when we get home, it will be very, very hard (probably impossible) for us to spend the time gathered with our brothers and sisters delighting in God and encouraging each other to do the same.

missionary shared a story of brutal and horrendous persecution, as well as incredible stories of gospel growth in the face of suffering. Most of the church was in tears, including me. Sadly, I'd spent most of the previous week pondering my next product purchase. What had monopolized my mind for days suddenly seemed like a complete waste of time.

The weekly practice of giving up our lives and ambitions to Jesus will not only reshape our weekly gatherings; it will also reshape the rest of our lives. We'll carry that recommitment from our gatherings out into everything that we do. We won't hang on so tightly to all our dreams and ambitions. We'll hold them loosely, if at all. Instead, our lives will be driven by the gospel, by joy in what God has done, by genuine rest in Jesus, and by delight in the presence of the Holy Spirit.

As we learn to let go, we'll find real rest—true rest. It won't be perfect rest; we won't taste that until Jesus returns to gather his people to himself. But it will be the best rest we can ever receive in this life—rest that's better than the best overseas holiday and better than the best experience we've ever had. It will cost us everything, but it is the greatest and most precious rest we can receive.

CONCLUSION:
LIVING AS GOD'S CHURCH

As discussed throughout this book, COVID has raised significant questions for churches. But many of these questions were already floating around beforehand. Questions about why we gather together and what it means to belong to a church. Questions about whether Christians really need to belong to a church at all. Questions about who serves, in what ways and where. Questions about how to sustain that service in the lives of busy people. The aim of this book has been to address some of those current questions but also to think deeply and biblically about God's purpose and plan for the church, so that we can think well about the church when new questions arise.

We've seen that we need to shift our expectations. We need to stop expecting things that aren't that important and start expecting things that are. We need to stop expecting certain facilities, programs, levels of relationship and levels of 'service'. We also need to be prepared for disappointments within our churches this side of eternity. Churches remain places where sinners gather together, which means they will always be places of disappointment and heartache. Yet we also need to start expecting, longing, praying and working for the right things: love, maturity in Christ, joy in God, and for the glory of God to be displayed in the church.

We also need to understand the story of the church. The church matters because it's a key part of God's plan of salvation for the world—God is saving a *people* for himself. God is reconciling and gathering a people to himself through the death of Jesus, recreating them in his image through the Spirit, uniting them into the family of God, and building them into a building in which God dwells. That means church is not a kind of optional extra for the Christian life; it's central and essential. Our identities as individual Christians grow out of the corporate identity we have in Christ and his body, not the other way around.

We need to be crystal clear on the church's purpose. The church is a community that lives out the Great Commandments and the Great Commission. It's a community that loves God with heart, soul, mind and strength, loves others, and makes disciples.

And we need to understand the mechanics of how the local church achieves its purpose. Because the local church is a reflection of all the believers already gathered around Jesus in the heavenly places, it is a community that regularly gathers to praise God, hear God speak in his word, apply God's word to our lives, pray, and be brought to maturity in Jesus. But it's a community that then scatters into the many and diverse places where God puts us. As we scatter, we take the gospel with us.

The church is a community equipped by God's Spirit to serve him and others, and it's a community of deep and profound rest amid a restless world—rest in the good news of what God has done in Jesus, rest in God's daily goodness, and rest from our own pursuits by laying down our lives daily at the feet of Jesus.

God loves his church. He loves it so much he sent his own Son to die to gather it into existence. It is one of his rich gifts to us. My prayer is that you will love the church as much as God loves it, and that you will receive it as a precious gift from God, however costly that may be for you to do.

ACKNOWLEDGEMENTS

The material in this book began life as a sermon series in 2012. Having only recently begun as the pastor of the Branch Christian Church in Launceston, Australia, I wanted to outline the Bible's model of what it means for us to be God's church. Since that original sermon series, the material has been further refined through teaching on the doctrine of the church for Reformed Theological College, Melbourne. Then, in the first year of the COVID pandemic, it seemed like a good time to revisit the material in another sermon series for the Branch. The material has thus been shaped by many people over quite a few years—people from the Branch, students from RTC, as well as numerous conversations with others.

Perhaps the greatest debt is owed to my friend and mentor, Peter Adam. It was through listening to many of his sermons and through conversations with him that my understanding of the church really began to take shape. His exposition of the Scriptures and his wisdom from many years of pastoring had an enormous impact on me and on the material here, especially on the first chapter on expectations. Apart from him, I might still have a very low view of the church.

I'm deeply appreciative to Matthias Media for their willingness to publish this book. Particular thanks must go to Geoff Robson—perhaps the most gracious editor I've ever worked with.

Thanks must also go to the many friends who constantly support me in life: Trent and Ange, Ant, Ollie, and Jed. It is their constant and astonishing kindness that has enabled me to write this book.

But this book is dedicated to my dear friend Achim. One could not ask for a kinder, more loving or more generous friend. Thanks mate, I'd be lost without you. I pray this book will help you and Janni to think wisely and biblically about what it means to serve God's church.

Feedback on this resource

We really appreciate getting feedback about our resources—not just suggestions for how to improve them, but also positive feedback and ways they can be used. We especially love to hear that the resources may have helped someone in their Christian growth.

You can send feedback to us via the 'Feedback' menu in our online store, or write to us at info@matthiasmedia.com.au.

❀matthiasmedia

Matthias Media is an evangelical publishing ministry that seeks to persuade all Christians of the truth of God's purposes in Jesus Christ as revealed in the Bible, and equip them with high-quality resources, so that by the work of the Holy Spirit they will:

- abandon their lives to the honour and service of Christ in daily holiness and decision-making
- pray constantly in Christ's name for the fruitfulness and growth of his gospel
- speak the Bible's life-changing word whenever and however they can—in the home, in the world and in the fellowship of his people.

Our resources range includes Bible studies, books, training courses, tracts and children's material. To find out more, and to access samples and free downloads, visit our website:

www.matthiasmedia.com

How to buy our resources

1. Direct from us over the internet:
   - in the US: www.matthiasmedia.com
   - in Australia: www.matthiasmedia.com.au

2. Direct from us by phone: please visit our website for current phone contact information.

3. Through a range of outlets in various parts of the world. Visit **www.matthiasmedia.com/contact** for details about recommended retailers in your part of the world.

4. Trade enquiries can be addressed to:
   - in the US and Canada: sales@matthiasmedia.com
   - in Australia and the rest of the world: sales@matthiasmedia.com.au

---

Register at our website for our **free** regular email update to receive information about the latest new resources, **exclusive special offers**, and free articles to help you grow in your Christian life and ministry.